Financial Post

GUIDE TO MUTUAL FUNDS

A Note on the Authors

Following several years as a staff writer for the *Financial Post*, John DeMont is currently a senior writer with *Maclean's*. He has written extensively on personal finance for such magazines as *Moneywise* and *Your Money*, as well as frequently appearing as a guest on Moneysworth.

Tracy LeMay is a Senior Editor at the *Post*, and has written for a wide variety of magazines, including *Moneywise*. Tracy has also been a consultant on TVO's personal finance show, Moneysworth.

Financial Post
GUIDE TO MUTUAL FUNDS

JOHN DeMONT and TRACY LeMAY

Random House
Toronto

Published in Canada in 1988 by Random House of Canada Limited, Toronto.

Canadian Cataloguing in Publication Data

DeMont, John
Financial post guide to mutual funds

Includes index.
ISBN 0-394-22066-8

1. Mutual funds - Canada. I. LeMay, Tracy.
II. Title.

HG5154.5.D45 1988 332.63'27 C88-094475-7

COVER DESIGN by Brant Cowie/Artplus Ltd.

Printed in Canada

The authors would like to thank the following people for their kind assistance: Toby Condliffe, Walwyn Stodgell Cochran Murray Limited; William J. Strain, Deloitte Haskins and Sells; Richard Hamm, Trimark Investment Management Incorporated; Tony De Thomasis, De Thomas Financial Corporation; and Robert Tattersall, Horgan Tattersall Investment Council Limited.

This book is up to date at the time of printing and has been verified by experts in various fields of personal money. However, the nature of some of the material covered may alter with changes in legislation, or to financial markets. Thus, while the book may be used as a basis for investment or special financial action, most people should consult professionals and seek their advice before proceeding on these matters.

Table of Contents

Introduction 1

CHAPTER 1
The Basics 19

CHAPTER 2
The Exotica 35

CHAPTER 3
Closed-end Funds 45

CHAPTER 4
Mutual Funds as Registered
Retirement Savings Plan Investments 53

CHAPTER 5
Playing the Game 61

CHAPTER 6
Picking the Right Fund 81

CHAPTER 7
Choosing the Right Strategy 91

CHAPTER 8
The Managers 101

CHAPTER 9
The Salespeople 123

CHAPTER 10
Looking Ahead 133

A Reader's Guide to the Financial Post's Mutual Fund Tables 141

APPENDIX
Tables 145

Index 170

Introduction

IN A LARGE, GEORGIAN-STYLE MANSION in Toronto's Rosedale area, a member of one of Canada's wealthiest families chats with his investment adviser. Over tea served in fine bone china, they work out a complex plan to shelter the client's considerable wealth from tax while providing an opportunity to make money by buying stocks, bonds and real estate. Three thousand miles away, in a kitchen in the heart of British Columbia, an experienced mutual-fund salesperson makes a strong pitch to a young couple. The husband is reticent and cautious; he has never owned stocks or bonds. He likes to keep his cash in a bank checking account. So the salesman tailors his song and dance and multicolored charts to the wife. By the time he leaves, two hours later, both husband and wife have purchased mutual funds.

The two scenes couldn't be more different. Yet they demonstrate how mutual funds – one of the hottest-selling investments anywhere – are helping to transform the nature of the modern investment world. Funds are flourishing and they are capitalism's great equalizer: they provide the young British Columbia couple with access to the same investment expertise as the millionaire from Rosedale. And they give both big and small investors an easier, and perhaps safer, way to play volatile stock and bond markets.

Mutual funds have not only fueled the stock-buying orgy, but they are also altering the structure of capital markets. Combined with powerful pension funds, which hold billions in stocks and bonds, and computer-aided "program traders," who can send stock-market indexes careening up and down, mutual-fund organizations are contributing to the institutionalization of global stock markets. In the process, the small guy gets squeezed out. Concludes one Toronto fund manager: "The little guy, if he decides to go solo in the stock market, will just be swept along by the tide."

Mutual funds haven't just come of age in the past three years – they've literally exploded onto the Canadian investment scene. By year-end 1987, roughly 2.2 million Canadians owned mutual funds, about double the number of owners in mid-1986. (By comparison, the last extensive share-ownership survey conducted in 1986 showed that 2.8 million Canadians owned common shares.) With nearly $31 billion in assets, the industry has grown six-fold in just five years.

A mutual fund pools the cash of many investors and uses it to buy large quantities of securities such as stocks, bonds, commodities and real-estate assets. Stripped to its basics, a mutual fund is a company with one purpose: to invest. The big attraction is that you don't have to worry about the daily ups and downs of the market: a professional, competent money manager looks after that. This management expertise puts the small investor, who couldn't afford to hire such market savvy, on the same footing as the experienced deep-pocketed investor.

Because a mutual fund buys the securities of many companies, it offers diversification – a cornerstone in any successful investment plan. The idea is to spread your savings among many different securities so that you won't be devastated by a big drop in one or two. To diversify by yourself, to properly spread the risks around, you'd probably need a minimum of $10,000. A mutual fund gives you better diversification at a fraction of the price.

What really sets mutual funds apart from other investments is that you don't have to worry about selling your securities into the open market. Shareholders have the right to cash out by submitting their shares to the fund itself for their net asset, or break-up, value. As a result, how much money you make depends entirely upon the performance of the fund's underlying portfolio of investments, and not on what other investors are willing to pay for your fund units. The redemption feature also insures that you can have easy access to your money.

Mutual funds, of course, aren't perfect investments. The flip side of diversification is that you can't hit the big time by holding that one stock that really takes off.

Funds are also wrong if you're looking for a short-term investment. Buying and selling to catch stock-market moves is costly, because in most cases you're paying commissions of five to nine percent up front each time you buy a fund. Besides, funds managers are professionals, but they are not infallible. Stock markets move in fairly regular five-year cycles. Because of the cycles, fund performance can fluctuate dramatically within short periods. Staying on board for a few years gives the fund manager time to weather the market downturns, and to profit during the good times.

So who buys mutual funds? People who are looking for a relatively inexpensive baptism into the stock or bond markets; small investors with a little cash who want professional management and lots of diversification; and people who are too busy, or disinterested, to do the necessary homework to make informed decisions about which stocks or bonds to buy. While it's hard to make general statements, there *is* a model of a modern Canadian mutual-fund investor. Research by Winnipeg-based Investors Group Incorporated, Canada's biggest mutual-fund marketer, shows that the average fund investor is between thirty-five and sixty-five, is college- or university-educated and has a household income of more than $35,000. About two-thirds are male, nearly ninety percent are English-speaking, and about forty percent of them live in Ontario.

Mutual funds are big with institutions, too. Trustees, retirement plans and the pension plans of unions, corporations, churches, hospitals and schools are pouring money into mutual funds.

Mutual funds aren't new. The first one was formed in Scotland in 1860 to spread the investment risks of buying bonds from several different issues. But the Foreign & Colonial Government Trust, founded in London eight years later, is generally considered the grandfather of them all. The trust's purpose, according to the original prospectus, was to provide "the investor of moderate means the same advantages as the large capitalist, in diminishing the risk of investing in foreign and colonial government stocks." Its original portfolio consisted of eighteen different bonds from fifteen different countries. Since then, the popularity of investment trusts in Britain has fluctuated sharply. Today, they're extremely popular.

The investment trust idea caught on like wildfire in the United States. During the roaring twenties, new investment companies were hitting the market almost daily. Most were "closed-end" funds, whose share values bore little resemblance to the value of the fund's assets. What is thought to be the first North American open-ended mutual-fund company, Massachusetts Investors Trust, was launched in Boston in 1924 with a handful of shareholders and a mere $50,000. But enthusiasm for investment trusts abruptly disappeared with the great crash of 1929.

In Canada, the history of mutual funds goes back to 1932, when Calvin Bullock Limited, a U.S. investment-fund management firm, launched Canadian Investment Fund. The concept hardly took the public by storm. By 1950, there were only ten Canadian funds, with assets totaling $70 million. The fund industry took a big step into the future in 1949 when Winnipeg-based Investors Group, which has about sixteen percent of today's market share, began offering mutual funds door-to-door and through its financial centers.

Throughout the 1950s funds grew slowly. They were considered safe instruments for the financially conservative. But in the early 1960s a not-so-subtle change occurred in the industry's investment philosophy. Talk of reasonable income and stability virtually disappeared from the industry's promotional literature, and the advantage of diversification was played down. A new aggressive approach arose as younger fund managers – most of whom couldn't remember 1929 – began investing in smaller, speculative stocks.

With these venture funds (also called "go-go funds")

turning in sizzling gains of seventy to eighty percent in a single year, industry assets swelled to nearly $3 billion by 1968. Hundreds of new sales agents, including stockbrokers, entered the funds business for the first time.

Then in 1969 the stock market went into a steep dive and the mutual-fund craze crashed. The go-gos lost money for the first time in years. A *Financial Post* survey in 1969 showed that only seven of one hundred and five Canadian mutual funds recorded gains. Novice investors, who had been attracted by promises of big profits, began to sell out in droves. Net redemptions (redemptions minus sales) for the forty-nine members of the Canadian Mutual Funds Association hit $29.5 million in 1970.

In 1971, the industry's image was further tainted by the systematic looting of one of the world's hottest fund organizations. Investors Overseas Services Limited had been incorporated in Toronto by a charismatic, self-made guru of people's capitalism named Bernie Cornfeld. At its peak, the IOS empire included 250 subsidiaries, 16,000 sales agents and $2.3 billion in assets. Today, liquidators are still trying to unravel one of the most baffling scandals in the history of international business.

Bernie Cornfeld was a flamboyant, pint-sized former Socialist who was born in Brooklyn during the Depression. He came to savor champagne, Hollywood starlets and a life style a maharajah might envy. He earned a master's degree at Columbia University, spent a year as a social worker in Philadelphia, then became a full-time mutual-fund sales agent in the 1960s.

In 1955, Cornfeld had taken a trip to Europe and decided to stay for good. In those days most Europeans knew little about mutual funds, and Cornfeld soon realized that investments in

U.S. securities could be sold to great numbers of Europeans, who had been putting their money into land or bank accounts. To avoid the risk of picking stocks for investment, he created the Fund of Funds, a mutual fund that buys the shares of other funds. Cornfeld knew of a curious legal loophole that allowed companies incorporated in Canada before 1965 and that carried on all their business overseas to avoid Canadian taxes. He would also gain the credibility of a Canadian address. So most of the funds were incorporated here.

Soon Cornfeld was hiring sales people and inspiring them with his own missionarylike zeal, which is epitomized by his challenge: "Do you sincerely want to be rich?" Cornfeld himself was living a princely existence. He divided his time between a fourteenth-century château in France, a lakeside villa in Geneva, a London town house and a modern, elegant hotel suite in New York. Cornfeld's 1970 Christmas present to the faithful was a $100,000 bash in Geneva's Intercontinental Hotel, where the guests drank three thousand bottles of Moet & Chandon champagne and every woman was given a scarf made by Paris fashion house Guy Laroche, in which Cornfeld had a personal investment.

But Cornfeld's world crumbled in 1971 when the stock market plummeted and IOS investors started cashing in their units as quickly as they could. With revenue from new sales dried up and expenses running as high as $20 million a quarter, IOS was suddenly bleeding to death. To the rescue with badly needed cash came Robert L. Vesco, a hefty, beady-eyed man from Detroit, an auto worker's son, who would eventually be known as one of the biggest swindlers in history. He had risen from obscurity by building a highly leveraged little-known conglomerate by the name of

International Controls Corporation. Vesco wanted international recognition, and the sudden crisis at IOS provided him with the perfect opportunity.

Cornfeld was no match for Vesco. First Vesco lent IOS $5 million – a sum which Vesco had to borrow. By 1971 he had absolute control of IOS, having bought Cornfeld out for a mere $5.5 million. Vesco was soon diverting IOS's assets into a maze of shell companies, dummy banks and secret numbered accounts from Costa Rica to the Bahamas. Vesco's chief aid and confidant was Norman Leblanc, a Montreal accountant who once won the governor-general's gold medal for the highest accounting marks in Canada. Though Canadian authorities didn't do much to stem the outflow of money from IOS headquarters in Saint John, New Brunswick, the U.S. authorities did. In 1971 the U.S. Securities and Exchange Commission issued charges of fraud totaling $225 million against Vesco, Leblanc and forty other defendants. But when the warrants were issued, Vesco and Leblanc had fled to Costa Rica. In 1973, IOS Limited, the parent company, was put into liquidation by the New Brunswick Supreme Court.

For the liquidators, tracing the lost millions has been an exercise in detective work and pure perseverance. But they've been remarkably successful in recovering investors' money, in some cases paying out dividends that exceeded the original investments. With most of the funds dismantled, their biggest problem is locating thousands of investors who are still owed dividends.

The key players in the scandal have scattered far and wide. Hardest to track down has been the shadowy Vesco, who is wanted for misappropriating U.S. $225 million in IOS funds and for allegedly making an illegal $200,000 contribution to former president Richard Nixon's 1972 election campaign. Since fleeing the United States, he's lived in, among other places, the Bahamas, Costa Rica and Grenada, and most recently was reported to be hanging his hat in Cuba, although Cuban authorities say they don't know his whereabouts. Holed up only five hundred miles from Cuba, in Costa Rica, is Norman Leblanc, now a well-paid financial adviser to some rich but unidentified Costa Rican businessmen.

In 1973, Cornfeld spent eleven months in a Swiss jail on fraud charges, of which he was eventually acquitted, stemming from the IOS collapse. When last heard from, he was comfortably ensconced in the mansion of Douglas Fairbanks, Jr., in Los Angeles, and was busy directing films and building a chain of health-food stores. The liquidators joke that Cornfeld should call the chain "Food of Foods."

The IOS fiasco dealt the funds business a near-fatal blow. Redemptions soared to $114.3 million for 1971. After redemptions swelled to $299 million in 1972, the Canadian Mutual Funds Association took the unprecedented step of halting the publication of embarrassing quarterly sales statistics. Even so, investors continued to dump more mutual-fund shares than they bought from 1973 to 1979.

Although stock markets recovered from the ten-year slump that began in 1969, it took years for mutual funds to regain credibility. Investors simply wanted better investment performance than that available from funds, many of which steadily underperformed the markets. There was also increasing pressure to reduce sales charges, which averaged about eight percent, as more and more people realized just how high front-end sales charges, or "loads," really were.

What has pushed mutual funds into the forefront in the 1980s? First, there were the rising stock markets. Before the October 1987 meltdown, the Toronto Stock Exchange's 300

Composite Index had topped 3,000 points, compared to less than 1,400 when the bull market began in 1982; the Dow Jones Industrial Average was more than 2,700, compared to less than 800 in 1982; and the Nikkea 225 stock average in Japan hit 26,600 compared to near 500. Mutual funds provided easy access to those markets. From 1984 to 1986, foreign funds – especially those specializing in the booming Japanese stock markets – topped the performance tables, sometimes gaining eighty or ninety percent in a single year.

But there's more to the sales boom than rising stock prices. The $500,000 lifetime capital-gains tax exemption, introduced in the 1985 federal budget, made capital gains more attractive. Although the exemption was cut back to $100,000 in 1987, it still provides a powerful incentive for investors to earn capital gains, compared to interest or dividend income.

Also, today people have more money to spend. Many families have two full-time salaries coming in. Years ago most extra money was tucked safely away in bank and trust-company deposits – but years ago, savings accounts paid double digit rates. In early 1987, they paid as low as four percent. People have understandably been looking for better harbors. "The maturing baby boomers simply have a better grasp of investing than their predecessors," says Toronto fund manager Bob Tattersall.

Not to be ignored is the big role aggressive marketing has played in the sales boom. In the past, when mutual funds were viewed as tame investments for conservative investors, the main sellers were independent sales agents and the fund organizations themselves. But lately, financial planners have been pushing their clients to buy mutual funds. As well, several trust companies and life-insurance firms have further legitimized the market by creating their own funds for distribution by staff. But the big marketing push has come from Canada's eleven thousand stockbrokers, who for years scorned funds mainly because of the low commissions they paid. Most brokerage houses now have their own mutual-fund departments, and brokers account for more than half of new sales in Canada.

A weighty arsenal of modern marketing tools has been deployed to ferret out new customers: extensive market research, mass mailings, aggressive telephone sales, promotional pep rallies – just about anything that will pull money from Canadians' well-stuffed mattresses.

Mutual-fund promoters have also been beating the bushes for new, attention-grabbing methods to sell their funds. Time was when buying a mutual fund was simple. You bought either an equity fund, which buys stocks of a number of different companies, for capital gains, or a bond fund to provide steady income. Today, the concept is the thing. Lured by visions of big sales dollars, all sorts of people are pushing new and often exotic funds. While the traditional products still dominate, there are now funds that invest in everything from options, commodities, convertible debentures and preferred shares to foreign securities, stocks in specific industries such as energy or technology, and even companies that meet certain ethical criteria. Says Wayne Walker, vice-president of sales for the Investors Group: "Whatever investors want, the industry will deliver."

Naturally, the sales boom is making the companies who sell and manage funds very, very rich. Trust and life-insurance companies have been in the sales business for years selling their own funds. In fact, some of the largest individual funds are managed by trust companies. As of March 31, 1988, Royal Trust's mortgage fund held more than $1 billion in assets, for instance. Royal and several other trust companies offer their customers a portfolio of several different funds and allow them to make low or no-cost transfers among investments. Trust companies and some banks, which are just getting into the sales arena, are trying to offer a broad range of services and products to cater to the financial needs of all their customers.

The biggest independent sales outfit is Regal Capital Planners Limited, which has 270 sales agents selling a wide variety of funds. During the boom, the best salespeople around could haul home $1 million in commissions a year. And mutual-fund management companies are prospering, too. These companies receive roughly one percent of the assets they manage. With industry assets swollen to $31 billion, that translates into roughly $310 million in revenues for 1987.

Investors Group Incorporated is one big fund-management company that prospered during the boom. Measured by assets, Investors Group of Winnipeg is Canada's largest marketer of mutual funds. Powered by a huge sales force that preaches a gospel of safety and security, Investors Group, which is controlled by Paul Desmarais's Power Financial Corporation, now has more than $5 billion in mutual-fund assets under administration. That's about sixteen percent of the domestic market, making it larger than the entire Canadian mutual-fund industry at the end of 1982.

Investors Group uses a far more conservative approach than its major competitors. While most fund companies depend on stockbrokers and independent dealers for sales, Investors Group has 1,900 of its own salespeople, who sell insurance, annuities, term deposits and other products as well as mutual funds. And, since 1978, Investors Group salespeople have been emphasizing their ability to supply integrated financial planning, as well as mutual funds and other products.

While most management companies depend upon hotshot performance gains for sales, Investors Group doesn't advertise its performance. Cynics suggest that's a good idea. With the exception of its Japan fund, Investors Group funds have been steady but hardly scintillating performers in the 1980s.

But by stressing safety rather than growth and by offering a wide range of conservative financial products, Investors Group thinks it will be well positioned even if Canadians' love affair with funds sours. Still, Investors Group, which went public in 1986, is doing its best to add a touch of dynamism to its stodgy image. Heading up the transition is Arthur Mauro, a thoughtful and articulate lawyer from Thunder Bay, Ontario. He chaired a Canadian royal commission on northern transport links in the 1960s and spent five years as president of Transair Limited (now Canadian Airlines International) before joining Investors Group in 1977. Investors is adding new funds, has bought into a broker dealer in the United States and is contemplating selling financial services in shopping centers. Perhaps the most tangible symbol of Investors Group's resurgent energy is a new head office in Winnipeg – a modern nineteen-story, $35 million building in the shape of a grain elevator, across town from its dowdy original headquarters.

The fastest-growing outfit is aggressive Toronto-based MacKenzie Financial Corporation. It has more than $3.7 billion in assets, and has captured nearly twelve percent of the Canadian market since starting from scratch a decade ago. MacKenzie has become the company to watch by doing the unconventional. It ignores the press, sponsors a high-powered Indy race car to raise its U.S. profile and rewards the independent brokers who sell its funds with exotic trips and special investment opportunities.

MacKenzie attracts investors' money mainly on the record of its five-person investment team, led by Alexander Christ, a shy, lean, stock-picking legend who was one of the first Harvard MBAs to work on Bay Street. Just as important to MacKenzie's success is the marketing prowess of its president, Jim O'Donnell. MacKenzie depends on stockbrokers and other independent sales agents to sell its funds. And O'Donnell has been a mastermind at building up loyalty in the brokerage business. Brokers have plenty of access to O'Donnell and Christ, and are provided with reams of information about MacKenzie's funds, which they can pass along to clients. MacKenzie also equips agents who have the best sales with their own computer terminals, so the agents can purchase funds directly for clients. In addition, MacKenzie pioneered the increasingly popular practice of flying its best sales agents to exotic locales, such as Rome and Sydney, each year for a few days of education and socializing.

What's next at MacKenzie? New funds with attractive fee structures, for one thing. And MacKenzie is also placing increased emphasis on its U.S. operation, headquartered in West Palm Beach, Florida. Says O'Donnell: "This is the age of specialization. We may try to provide additional investment products within the existing framework, but our job will remain managing money."

AGF Management Limited, based in Toronto, controls $2.7 billion in assets, or about nine percent of the market. AGF has captured its share of the industry by trying to be everything to everyone. With twenty funds in its stable, AGF offers more options than any Canadian fund outfit – everything from high-technology funds, energy funds and Japanese funds to bonds, money-market instruments and stock indexes. But what really corrals investor money is that AGF's funds perform.

Consistency is AGF's forte. During the decade ending March 31, 1988, the best-performing Canadian-based fund was AGF Japan Fund, up an average of 23.5% annually. Fourth-best overall during that period was AGF Special Fund, up an average of 21.8% annually. Management, naturally, is the key. Unlike many organizations, which make investment decisions by committee, AGF's managers succeed or fail on their own. And AGF's stock pickers have been singling out winners for years. Chairman Warren Goldring has been running AGF's fixed-income funds for twenty-five years; Bill Cameron has been guiding the foreign funds since the late 1960s; Robert Farquharson has been managing the Canadian equity funds and AGF's gas and energy fund for twenty-four years; and Richard Whiting has headed the special and high-tech funds for fifteen years.

Because of its wide menu of funds, AGF's 285,000 clients range from the small investor, who can only scrape together the $1,000 minimum, to big players, like one family trust that has sunk $42 million into AGF funds.

The mutual-funds boom has attracted lots of new players into the game. Most have made successful entrances, but there have been some notable flops. Brokerage house Walwyn Stodgell Cochran Murray Limited tried to jump on the money wagon with seven new funds in the summer of 1987. By March 1988 Walwyn had only attracted $70 million in assets, and it decided to sell out to a money management firm, BPI Capital Corporation.

Even more disheartening was the experience of Hume

Group Limited, which publishes and sells home-study investment courses and *The MoneyLetter*, a widely read investment newsletter. The Hume Group hired several high-profile investment luminaries to run its funds, including Toronto investor and arbitrager Andy Sarlos; Norman Short, president of mutual-fund company Guardian Capital Group Limited; Toronto money manager Fred McCutcheon; and flamboyant author, physician and investor Morton Shulman. But the funds were dismal performers after they hit the market in mid-1985 – no doubt a source of great embarrassment to the Hume team. In March 1988, Hume sold control of the funds to a venture capital firm called Altamira Management Limited.

The exponential growth of mutual funds has left even seasoned industry pros shaking their heads in disbelief. In 1985 Bob Stewart, president of Dynamic Funds Management Incorporated and chairman of the Investment Funds Institute of Canada, predicted $20 billion in industry assets by 1990. But we've already topped $30 billion, in spite of the October 1987 crash.

And there's probably room to grow. Compared to twenty-four percent of households in the United States, it is estimated that only twelve percent of Canadian households currently own mutual funds. Moreover, Ottawa has proposed to make pension plans portable and to increase maximum contributions to registered retirement savings plans, which should ensure a steady flow of cash into mutual funds.

The mutual-funds industry is affected by changes in Canada's financial-services sector. The "Little Bang" in 1987 in Ontario's financial-services industry allows foreign mutual-fund dealers to set up Canadian subsidiaries to manage and publicly distribute Canadian-registered funds. As for the established players, they must respond to the challenge with new services and products, or they will stagnate.

How do you, as a new investor, sort through all the marketing hype, the perplexing array of exotic new products and players to decide which fund to buy? That's where this book comes in. Despite the dramatic changes in the Canadian fund business, investing in mutual funds doesn't have to be complicated – but you have to be smart. With a bit of homework, and a thorough read of the *Financial Post Guide to Mutual Funds*, you should do as well as any broker or independent sales agent when you pick your fund. To make the task even easier, we've included the *Financial Post*'s exclusive mutual-funds tables, which contain all the hard numbers you'll need to assess performances. So read on.

Chapter 1

The Basics

THE NUMBER OF SELECTIONS on the mutual-fund program is big and rapidly growing bigger. And as the number of funds grows, so does the complexity of the marketplace. That means that nabbing the most appropriate funds is a challenging job. To help you along, here's a roundup of major fund types.

Stock Funds

There are two ways to buy stocks. You can find yourself a level-headed, ethical, experienced broker who knows how to pick the stocks that will fatten your portfolio. But buying stocks alone is risky, and unless you've got more than $100,000 to invest, you'll have a hard time obtaining the best advice. The simplest – and safest – way to reduce some of the risk is to invest in a professionally managed equity fund, where your money is pooled to buy a selection of different stocks. Instead of personally having to pick stocks to buy and sell, you pay an experienced money manager to make those decisions. All you have to do is select which funds to invest in, how much and when. Leave the rest to the manager.

Equity funds or stock funds allow you to spread the considerable risks of playing the stock market. Let's say you, as an individual, buy shares in Moosepasture Mines Incorporated. You stand to make a fortune if the shares go from $10 to $50. But what if they fall to $1? If you had, say, a quarter of your savings in Moosepasture Mines, you'd suddenly find yourself dining on Hamburger Helper instead of haute cuisine.

If you buy into a stock fund, you buy diversification, one of the fundamentals of prudent stock-market investing and a key attraction of mutual funds. The idea is to spread your risk across a range of securities, to soothe the blow if one stock self-destructs. Unless you have $100,000 or so to invest, you really can't hold enough different stocks to reduce your risks to a manageable level.

But equity mutual funds diversify among dozens, or even hundreds, of different securities. As most funds also invest among many different industries, you are protected if one sector of the economy slumps. If your fund had, say, one percent of its equity in Moosepasture Mines and the rest in fifty or a hundred other stocks in a wide range of other industries, you'd only lose a bit if Moosepasture were to nosedive. Chances are, though, that while Moosepasture falls, other stocks in your fund are moving in the other direction. In theory, they should more than make up for the Moosepasture loss.

Of course, if Moosepasture skyrocketed your fund wouldn't benefit much from the move. That's the price you have to pay for diversification. The average Canadian stock fund, in fact, failed to keep up with the market during the past decade. Generally speaking, you would have been better off buying the stocks listed in the Toronto Stock Exchange 300 Composite Index. During the decade ended March 31, 1988, the TSE's total returns index (TSE 300 and reinvested dividends) gained an average of 16.5% while the average Canadian equity fund gained only 13.8%.

Nobody, of course, buys the "average fund," and a number of funds did spectacularly better than the average. Among the big winners were funds that invested globally, particularly in the booming Japanese markets. During the past five years, Japanese funds were up an average of 34%, compared to 12.6% for the TSE. Newer funds that started in the midst of the stock boom also prospered, mainly because they were starting from a smaller base.

Why did many funds fail to keep up with the bull market? Some mutual-fund managers made tactical errors. Many of them focused too heavily on small companies rather than big-capitalization stocks. The foreign money that drove our markets in 1986 and 1987 was mainly directed at bigger, better-known stocks.

Other managers were out of the resource industry when these shares caught fire in 1986. As well, during 1986 and 1987 many funds built up big cash reserves because money poured in faster than managers could invest it. This hefty cash component hurt performance, because treasury bills and other similar investments have had relatively low yields, compared to many equity investments. (Still, many of these cash-heavy managers looked like geniuses in October 1987, when the crash came. Cash investments may not provide spectacular returns but they are more lucrative than falling stocks.) Finally, there was also lots of turnover in management during this period; changing strategy in midstream hurt some funds.

When the crash came, equity funds were hit particularly hard in spite of their diversification. In the four months after the 1987 crash, Canadian equity funds gained an average of just 4.9%, and some did much worse. Since common stock prices are typically more volatile than the prices of other types of securities, equity fund prices usually fluctuate widely. Generally, they should outperform other types of funds in a rising stock market, and fall off more quickly when the market drops.

How a fund ultimately performs depends upon what a manager buys, sells and holds in the portfolio. Most equity funds face similar restrictions: a maximum of ten percent can be invested in the shares or other securities of a single company. Fund managers aren't allowed to sell short – that is, sell securities the fund doesn't own in the hope of being able to buy them back later at lower prices. Also forbidden is buying stocks on margin – using borrowed money to buy securities, and assigning the securities to the lender as collateral for the loan – and buying or selling commodity futures contracts. Fund managers are also allowed only limited use of options to protect against declines in the value of the portfolio. Other than that, the fund manager pretty much has a free hand.

Even among funds whose objectives are the same, there is room for individuality. Some fund managers take a "top-down" approach to investment. They first determine the major forces affecting the economy and the investment markets – inflation, the value of the dollar, interest rates – and then look for shares in industry groups or sectors that will benefit by rising in value or yielding attractive dividends. Others take a "bottom-up" approach, conducting detailed research about particular companies and looking for underpriced shares. Some like to hold shares for long periods, while others prefer to trade frequently, with the dollar value of the trades sometimes exceeding the fund's assets under administration in a single year.

Fund performance, as a result, is just as idiosyncratic. Certain types of funds perform differently in different stock-market and economic cycles. Managers, for instance, who invest only in undervalued stocks usually underperform the averages in a full-fledged bull market where share prices are galloping way ahead of earnings, and when there are few stocks that fit their criteria. In the same way, aggressive growth funds may sink farther than more conservative funds when the stock market stalls.

There are myriad equity funds, ranging from conservative funds that invest in well-known, blue-chip stocks, to exotic funds specializing in foreign investments. We'll deal with the exotica in the next chapter. For now, here's a look at the two most popular types: aggressive growth funds and blue-chip equity funds.

Growth funds

When stock prices are roaring ahead, some of the best-performing funds tend to be aggressive growth funds, which pursue maximum profits by buying shares in companies loaded with growth potential at the expense of current dividends. These funds are often easily identified by their descriptive names, such as Multiple Opportunities Fund, United Venture Fund, Principal Speculators Fund and so on. Usually, fund managers scout for small companies in new fields that hint of real promise but don't yet have much in the way of earnings. They may also invest in turnaround situations, taking gambles on companies that have fallen on hard times but that could return to their former glory.

As a result, these funds tend to hold loads of stocks in smaller companies with shorter track records, companies involved in start-up projects as well as securities listed on more speculative exchanges like the Vancouver Stock Exchange. But the stock market doesn't yield big returns easily. While growth funds tend to rise the quickest, they also flame out faster than the rest, so you have to be prepared to get mauled during a bear market. Consider the go-go funds of the 1960s, when a number of managers invested large portions of their portfolios in less well-known issues, especially electronics and resource company stocks. Many of the gains were wiped out when the market broke in 1969. The experience was repeated after the 1987 crash. Look at Multiple Opportunities Fund, which was up 122% for the twelve months ending July 31, 1987, after making a killing on speculative Vancouver Stock Exchange-listed gold and industrial companies. But it lost 30% in the six months ending February 28, 1988.

Still, there are a few aggressive growth funds that have managed to turn in steady returns despite their speculative bent. One of the best is AGF Special Fund, which searches for what it calls "special situations" among speculative stocks. The fund has managed to gain an average 21.8% annually during the decade ended March 31, 1988. That made it the fifth-best performer among Canadian funds.

Blue-chip equity funds

If aggressive funds are a bit too risky for your blood, there are plenty of middle-of-the-road equity funds. They buy higher-quality, blue-chip securities but still offer the potential for a steady, long-term increase in capital. Usually these funds describe their investment goals as something like "to provide unit holders with professional investment management to obtain a reasonable return on investment capital and long-term capital appreciation consistent with safety of principal." Translation: these funds usually steer clear of speculative new issues and companies without proven records of profitability.

Instead, their holdings are in large, well-known corporations with good track records and steady dividend payments – household names like Canadian Pacific, Bell Canada Enterprises and Canadian banks. They are also quite prepared to move into treasury bills and other short-term money-market instruments when the stock market looks risky.

As their portfolios often mirror the Toronto Stock Exchange's 300 Composite Index, they tend to follow overall market trends. As a result, they stand to be far less volatile than growth funds. Thus they are good investments for people with long-term goals who are willing to assume some risk in the quest for greater rewards.

The best of the lot have managed to show remarkable consistency during both good and bad markets. Cundill Value Fund, managed by the irrepressible Peter Cundill, was up an average of 21.2% annually during the decade ended March 31, 1988. With publicity-shy Alexander Christ, chairman of MacKenzie Financial Corporation at the helm, MacKenzie Equity Fund and Industrial Growth Fund were up an average of 19.5% each year and 17.8% each year for the past ten years. Then there's Templeton Growth Fund, managed by the august John Templeton, up 17.3% annually in ten years. And the Royal Bank of Canada's unheralded Royfund Equity Fund, run by Martin Siegerman, has climbed 18.4% a year during the past decade.

Fixed-income funds

Perhaps the thought of putting your cash into more volatile stocks makes your hair fall out in wispy tufts. Or maybe you're convinced that stock prices are going to be as flat as a chunk of prairie landscape sometime into the next millenium. Then it's time to emphasize safety and income through fixed-income investments that bypass the stock market completely. Without professional help, going for yield by yourself isn't easy. And you would also need loads of cash to play the fixed-income game alone, since you have to make a bigger initial investment here than in the stock market.

That's where professionally managed fixed-income mutual funds come in handy. These funds invest in fixed-income securities like short-term money-market instruments, mortgages and long-term government bonds. That conservative strategy may make lousy party chitchat – but if it's excitement you're after, try the growth funds.

Income-spinning funds are about as close as most of us will get to a sure thing. Although they may be a tad tame for your blood, fixed-income funds should have a place in every prudent investor's portfolio. Besides, if you're willing to handle a bit more volatility, you get some capital-gains potential.

In theory, fixed-income fund managers pick the most suitable investments and provide much greater diversification than you could on your own. As interest rates have fallen in the past few years, liquid assets have flowed, some would say flooded, into fixed-income funds. In March 1988, the Investment Funds Institute of Canada (IFIC) reported that funds investing for income – those that hold bonds, mortgages and money-market instruments – had a total value of $7 billion. Canadian equity funds, excluding preferred share funds, had assets of $6.9 billion.

The fixed-income list is long and getting longer. There are four main categories of fixed-income investments: money-market funds, mortgage funds, bond funds and dividend funds. Sorting through the list of possibilities involves as much planning and expertise as buying a stock fund.

As usual, you need to define your objectives. And remember

that different types of income funds pose varying degrees of risk. The funds may fluctuate in value depending on the terms of securities, the relationship of their rate of return to market interest rates and the financial stability of the issuing government or corporation.

Money-market funds

Money-market funds, as their name suggests, invest in the huge international marketplace of IOUs that makes up the money market. It is here that governments, corporations and banks borrow money, for several months or for a few hours.

These low-risk, short-term securities – which usually mature in less than ninety days – pay steady interest, but provide little in the way of opportunities for capital gains (or losses). Investments include government treasury bills, certificates of deposit, bankers' acceptances (promissory notes issued by corporations, but guaranteed by chartered banks) and A-rated corporate paper.

Because they invest in short-term instruments, interest paid by money-market funds reflects the price of short-term money. (But, as a practical matter, most money-market funds are structured so that the unit value is fixed at a specific price regardless of changes in interest rates.) Maneuverability is the key: if interest rates rise, the fund manager can capitalize swiftly by rolling the funds into the higher-interest-rate investments. The negative is that interest-rate declines will be quickly reflected in your return.

Think of money-market funds as high-interest-paying bank accounts. The only difference is that, unlike bank accounts, the funds aren't protected by the Canadian Deposit Insurance Corporation (CDIC), which guarantees deposits up to $60,000 per person per institution. But the securities the funds buy entail very little risk. Like a bank, money-market funds accept your money and offer complete liquidity. You can cash out anytime. You can't do this with certificates of deposit and other fixed-period vehicles.

When interest rates are high, money-market funds are perhaps the single best place to keep cash liquid. Usually you don't have to pay a fee to buy into the fund. That's understandable, as you're getting next to nothing in the way of investment advice. Service fees are normally charged on money-market funds to pay for the daily calculations of interest on your fund units, but these are negligible.

Because the funds diversify their investments by buying the paper of many different companies and government agencies, they typically pay higher rates than the bank. And they also offer a higher degree of safety than an isolated individual investment in the money market.

Who invests in money-market funds? Everyone from large corporations to people like you or me looking for a parking spot for cash between investments. If you want to be able to move your money around easily, the most convenient money-market funds may be those managed by mutual-fund families like Investors Group, Bolton Tremblay, AGF, Allied and others, which provide free switching in and out of their money-market funds.

Mortgage funds

Mortgage funds, which invest in both residential and commercial mortgages, are the middle ground for investors. They offer a higher rate of return than money-market funds, but do not have the risk of volatile, long-term bond funds.

Typically, mortgage funds invest in residential loans with terms of less than five years and commercial mortgages with terms of less than ten years. As a result, when interest rates change, the value of the portfolios usually fluctuates more than a shorter-term money-market fund and less than the longer-term bond funds.

Capital gains are possible, but these funds are mainly for income-seeking investors. The fund managers look at how prevailing mortgage rates compare to government of Canada bonds before deciding how to split up the fund's assets.

Diversification is the key. Managers try to spread the risk by varying the type, term and location of mortgaged properties. The tradeoff is that there's more risk with a mortgage fund than with a guaranteed investment certificate (GIC) or government of Canada bond. Although mortgages are saleable in a secondary market, they are not as liquid as bonds and money-market instruments. And there is always the risk of mortgage defaults, in which case assets would have to be sold, possibly at a loss, to cover the loan. (That's rare, as mortgage funds are usually offered by the trust companies who originally issue the mortgages. And many of the mortgages are insured by the Canada Mortgage and Housing Corporation.) Another negative is that the investment management fee on a mortgage fund is often somewhat higher than on other funds, because of greater administration costs. This eats into your yield.

Bond funds

If you can handle greater volatility, with the possibility of higher returns, a bond fund may be appropriate. These funds invest in bonds issued by provinces, the federal government and big, credit-worthy corporations. A bond is essentially a loan to a government or corporation where the lender – in this case the fund – is paid an annual interest rate and receives the principal back when the bond matures.

The fund manager's biggest concern is where interest rates are going. When rates rise, bond prices fall; when rates drop, prices increase. There is nothing mysterious about this. Let's say your manager paid $1,000 for a bond that yielded five percent a year. If interest rates increased so that newly issued bonds were yielding seven percent, then the price of your bond drops. Why would anyone pay $1,000 to buy your bond, which yields five percent, when other bonds yield seven?

Bond funds allow you to diversify among lots of different bonds with varying maturities, which is good. After all, it is just as risky to put all your money into bonds of one maturity as it is to put all your money into bonds of one company or government.

When considering which bond fund to buy, be aware of your own risk tolerance and investment time frame. You should also understand the investment policy of the fund, including the average term and quality of the bonds, the mix of foreign and domestic bonds and the management's track record. Ideally, what you're looking for is a fund that can steer through both rising and falling interest rates.

Dividend funds

For the investor who wants income, but also wants to keep a toe in the equity market, there are funds that invest mainly in dividend-paying preferred shares. These shares pay a dividend that rarely goes up, no matter how prosperous the company becomes. The nice thing is that the dividend won't go down, either, unless things really get desperate for the company. Most dividend funds are "cumulative preferreds." This means that if a dividend payment is omitted, the unpaid dividends accumulate and must go to preferred investors before common shareholders get a single penny. There are also other preferred wrinkles, including "convertibles," which can be switched into common shares.

There's a big tax advantage to receiving dividend income (compared to interest income), although the advantage has declined because of Ottawa's 1987 tax reform. But despite the reduction in the dividend tax credit, dividends still receive preferred tax treatment compared to interest income. As of May 1988, dividends from taxable Canadian corporations are "grossed up" by 25%, and the taxpayer receives a tax credit of 13.5% of the grossed-up amount.

Dividend funds tend to be less volatile than pure equity funds, because the dividend yields support the preferred stock's value. However, they are also sensitive to interest-rate changes. If interest rates rise, the value of the shares in the fund will fall because the dividend doesn't change. But to counterbalance, preferreds also offer capital-gains potential if the shares rise in value in response to a decline in interest rates.

Balanced funds

Balanced funds, which hold both equity and fixed-income securities, give you the best of both worlds: they try to hold enough bonds and preferred shares to offset fluctuations in their holdings of common stocks. And their common shares offer capital-gains potential seldom available from a fixed-income portfolio. Balanced funds provide a higher level of current income than, say, a straight common-stock fund. But there's usually less capital-gains potential. Over the long term, the net asset value of a balanced fund can be expected to lag behind a common-stock fund in a rising market, and to drop less when the market is falling.

The portfolio manager's job is to look at market conditions and juggle the mix of investments accordingly, raising the fixed-income portion in expectation of falling interest rates and moving into stocks when it looks like a bull market is about to appear. Usually managers try to keep the portfolio split as equally as possible between stocks and fixed-income instruments. But if there's a major change in the stock or bond markets, the asset mix can change dramatically.

Once the fund manager decides how to split up the portfolio, the next step is to pick which stocks and bonds to hold. A good manager will spread the risks among shares in different industries and geographic regions; the term and quality of bonds are varied to take advantage of both rising and falling interest rates. A number of balanced funds have managed to stay near the top of the performance tables in the past decade.

Chapter
2
The Exotica

PICKING A MUTUAL FUND was easy a few years ago, when most funds invested only in North American stocks and bonds. In recent years, though, there's been a veritable explosion of new, specialized products designed to tempt investors with even the most specific needs. The menu is now sprinkled with funds that invest in such things as real estate, precious metals and futures and options, as well as companies that measure up to strict ethical or moral guidelines. Particularly popular are funds that invest in specific types of industries or companies. They've enjoyed stunning performance gains during the 1980s. Those that sink their money into Japanese securities, for instance, have topped the performance tables in the past decade. Funds that invest in countries in Europe and the Pacific Rim have also been near the head of the pack.

But specialized funds carry their own special caveats. For example, at least half the performance gains made by the high-flying Japanese funds during the past five years were caused by exchange-rate fluctuations rather than by the performance of the underlying companies. But exchange rates can just as easily move against you. Meanwhile, funds that put money in a specific industry, say energy or mining, will be hit hard if the industry heads into a recession. But specialty funds can still be big winners.

Ethical funds

If you're the type of person who wants to put your money where your morals are, ethical funds are the way to go. These funds invest only in companies that pass specific ethical tests, which vary from fund to fund. The Ethical Growth Fund of the Vancouver City Savings Credit Union (Vancity), for instance, invests only in Canadian companies with good industrial relations and eschews those that give money to repressive government regimes, that make military goods or that profit from nuclear energy. Summa Fund Limited, managed by Winnipeg-based Investors Group Limited, uses a similar stock screen, but also sifts out companies linked with tobacco, alcohol and pornography. These restrictions aren't as limiting as you might think. Vancity's criteria, for instance, eliminate only forty or forty-five companies from the three hundred that make up the TSE's composite index.

The philosophical underpinning of ethical investing is that good corporate performance partly depends on good corporate conduct. After all, a company that is acting responsibly is less likely to run into problems stemming from questionable corporate activities. If you want confirmation of this thesis, look at the big drop in shares of A.H. Robins Company Incorporated as a result of the controversy surrounding the Dalkon Shield, one of its birth-control products. Or consider the asbestosis scandal, which helped to drive Manville Corporation into financial turmoil.

But, while popular in the United States, ethical funds are just starting to catch on in Canada. The handful of funds here have attracted far less attention than their U.S. counterparts.

So far, performance has been fairly good. But because of the short performance record, the jury is still out on this group. You might be wise to devote only a small percentage of your fund portfolio to ethical funds – at least until they establish a longer track record.

Real-estate funds

These funds held little lure for investors during the grand bull market, which continued until October 1987. After all, their performance had been anemic compared to the dazzling performance of equity funds during that period. But it was a different story after October nineteenth. While holders of equity funds suffered heavily, real-estate fund holders emerged unscathed, underlining the fact that these little-understood funds may have an important place in the portfolios of investors looking for shelter from volatile stock markets.

Real-estate funds mainly buy commercial, income-producing properties, such as shopping centers and industrial space. Income is derived from two major sources: the rent from tenants, and capital gains when the properties are sold.

These funds aren't designed for making a quick killing. The managers invest in properties for the long term. And it takes considerable time to build up a portfolio of good income-producing commercial and industrial properties.

The big attraction of real-estate funds is that they allow ordinary investors to participate in big-time real-estate investments, which are generally the preserve of corporations and high-rolling individuals. Minimum investments range from $2,500 at Investors Real Property Fund offered by Winnipeg-based Investors Group Incorporated to $500 for Imperial Realty Growth Fund, managed by Imperial Advisors Limited, also of Winnipeg.

The fund manager's job is to look for properties that offer steady income and capital-gains potential. Managers also try to diversify by type of property and geographic location, to avoid getting hammered if the real-estate market in a particular area slumps.

But real-estate funds aren't without risks. For one thing, performance figures may be somewhat deceptive as many of the funds haven't been in existence long enough to have faced downturns in the real-estate market.

An even bigger worry could be redeeming your fund investment. Consider what happened to Real Property Trust in 1985 when the value of its real-estate assets was written down. This shook investor confidence and triggered a flood of redemptions. The fund couldn't sell properties quickly enough to meet redemption demands. After a lengthy redemption freeze, unit holders voted in 1988 to wind up the fund and distribute the proceeds among themselves.

To avoid a repetition of the Real Property situation, fund managers are now required to maintain a ten-percent cash reserve. But even this might not be enough if a fund faces a rapid drop in real-estate prices.

Sector funds

Another way to win big is through sector funds, which enable investors to concentrate on the stocks of specific industries, such as health care, technology, energy or small-capitalization companies, without having to pick individual shares. Sector funds are a red-hot item in the bigger, more sophisticated U.S. fund market, but they have yet to catch on here. The biggest Canadian player is FutureFund Shares Incorporated of Ancaster, Ontario, which markets seven no-load sector funds: FoodFund, GoldenFund, LifeFund, TechnoFund, SilverFund, ValueFund and Natural Resources Fund. Interest in sector funds is so scant that in the summer of 1987 Guardian Capital Group Limited was forced to pull five sector funds it had launched just two years earlier.

Still, sector funds can provide good investment opportunities, as long as you are choosy. These funds provide two advantages of the traditional, broad-based mutual fund – the protection of diversification and the expertise of a professional money manager – without sacrificing investment specificity. They're good for investors who feel certain they know which stock groups will do well, but who aren't willing to gamble on one or two stocks.

While some of these funds turn in stunning performances, others flop dismally. Sector funds tend to concentrate their assets in a single area, which runs contrary to one of the tenets of successful fund investing. And, perhaps more importantly, an industry that is in vogue or performing particularly well one month may fall on hard times six months later.

Global funds

Consider global mutual funds if you want to play exotic foreign stock markets; they may be the only way for you to participate in the global action. If you try to invest outside Canada on your own you'll probably have difficulty finding a broker or adviser with first-hand knowledge of foreign markets. But by buying a global fund you can benefit from the experience of European, American and Asian managers who are paid to maneuver in the global marketplace.

International funds, as their name implies, allow you to spread your risk around the world. Studies have shown that a properly diversified international portfolio will outperform a strictly domestic one in the long run. For instance, the 12.6% gain recorded by the Toronto Stock Exchange's total returns index (TSE 300 Composite Index plus reinvested dividends) for the five years ending March 31, 1988, looks pretty paltry alongside the 22.1% gain registered by the Morgan Stanley Capital International World Index (the weighted average gain of approximately 1,900 securities listed on exchanges throughout the world) during the same period.

There are three types of worldwide funds: international funds, which invest in the securities of foreign countries; global funds, which invest in the securities of foreign countries as well as in the country in which the fund is based; and one-country funds, which invest in the securities of a single foreign country.

In recent years, one-country funds, particularly those that stress Japan, have been among the hottest performers. AGF Japan Fund, for instance, was up an average of 35.2% annually during the past five years, the best performance of any Canadian fund. Close behind was Investors Japan Fund, which climbed an average of 32.2% annually.

There are a number of fund managers with proven abilities to pick the right foreign markets. Bolton Tremblay International Fund, run by Bob Krembil from 1978 to 1986 and then by Peter Spark, was up an average 19.6% annually in those ten years. United Accumulative Fund, managed by well-respected Gerald Coleman of United Financial Management of Toronto, has gained an average of 18.7% annually for the past ten years. Templeton Growth Fund was up an average 17.3% annually in the past decade. And Eaton Group's Viking International Fund managed to rise by an average of 16.7% annually in ten years.

Remember that, although an international fund may outperform the TSE 300 Composite Index, the real question is how it does against competition in the international marketplace.

Investors dipping their toes into international markets should be aware of the risks involved. Just as foreign markets have outpaced North American stocks on the way up, they may also move faster on the way down. Also, if the Canadian dollar rises, currency gains quickly turn to currency losses, and the international situation suddenly doesn't look so rosy. Political crises and exchange controls are among the risks that mutual-fund investors need to consider.

Index funds

It doesn't always take a good manager to produce good mutual-fund returns. In fact, some funds have performed impressively without being actively managed at all. These are index funds, and their portfolios duplicate the makeup of a particular stock or bond index, such as the Toronto Stock Exchange 300 Composite Index, which is used to measure the health of the Toronto stock market.

The most common type of index fund, the stock index fund, invests in the companies that make up the index it imitates in the same proportion the companies are weighted in the index. Performance, as a result, mirrors the market average. But keeping pace with the averages isn't as easy as it sounds. For example, the average Canadian equity fund showed an annual 13.8% return in the past ten years, while the average U.S. equity fund sold in Canada had a 14.5% return. Meanwhile, the TSE total return index showed a 16.5% return over the same period. The Standard and Poor's 500 index did worse than the average U.S. fund, showing an 11.4% return.

But index funds have clear limitations. In a soaring bull market they may make many professional managers look bad, but when stock prices fall, these passively managed funds follow in lock step. And in a flat market you won't see much in the way of gains.

Index funds have proliferated in the United States, where they are widely used by pension funds. But so far there are only a few in Canada. Toronto-Dominion Bank sponsors two of them: the Green Line Canadian Index Fund, which holds the three hundred blue-chip stocks that make up the TSE's Composite Index; and the Green Line U.S. Index Fund, based on Standard and Poor's five hundred indexed stocks. The Bank of Montreal has the First Canadian Equity Index Fund, also based on the TSE 300. Royal Trust has introduced its Government Bond Index Fund, which mirrors brokerage house ScotiaMcLeod's long-term government-bond index. And Trafalgar Capital Management, a Toronto-based pension fund manager, introduced a pooled fund for pension managers based on the Europe, Australia and Far East Index published by Morgan, Stanley Capital International for investors seeking global exposure.

Chapter
3

Closed-end Funds

WHILE THEY CLOSELY RESEMBLE mutual funds, closed-end funds, are far different.

First, closed-end shares can be bought or sold either on a listed exchange or over the counter like any stock. Usually only a specific number of shares are issued in an initial offering. They may, however, issue additional shares as the managers see fit. In contrast, mutual-fund units don't trade on public exchanges like stocks or bonds. You simply buy units from the mutual-fund management company. Mutual-funds, as a result, expand or shrink depending on investor demand.

That's not all that's different. The value of your mutual-fund investment corresponds to the value of the underlying investments held by the fund. When you want to cash out, you simply return your units to the fund organization and receive their underlying asset value.

The value of closed-end fund units, on the other hand, is a

function not only of net asset value, but also of how investors feel about a particular fund. As a result, closed-end fund prices almost always diverge from their net asset value, occasionally commanding a "premium" above their asset value, but usually trading below the underlying value, or at a "discount."

There are loads of theories for the discounts, for example that these shares are "thin traders" and lack "sponsorship," or recommendations by brokerage houses. As an investor, all you have to know is that when it comes to closed-end funds there are two distinct price factors to consider: the increase or decrease in value of the underlying portfolio (just like in a mutual fund); and demand for the shares.

In theory, closed-end fund managers should have an easier time than mutual-fund managers in turning in good results. Closed-end fund managers get around a difficult problem the mutual-fund managers sometimes face. When stock markets are booming, investors tend to buy lots of mutual-fund units. That means managers have to find suitable investments for the cash flowing in, which might not be an easy job when stock values are peaking. Then, when the market drops, many investors redeem their units, forcing managers to sell stocks at greatly reduced prices. These pressures can play havoc with even the best of investment plans. But closed-end funds have a set amount of capital outstanding, so managers don't have to worry about coping with a big inflow of money when stock prices are high and a corresponding outflow when prices are low.

The first closed-end fund was launched in the early 1800s by King William I of the Netherlands. But their heyday came when people invested millions during the roaring twenties in the United States. The sales boom, however, came to an abrupt halt in 1929, when closed funds collapsed even more frightfully than the rest of the stock market. They are only now beginning to recover. In 1983, funds with a capitalization of U.S. $58 million hit the American market. That figure climbed to $106 million in 1984, $614 million in 1985, $5.3 billion in 1986 and $11 billion in 1987. The 1987 crash didn't cool off the closed-end fund market in the United States; seven funds with a capitalization of $5.5 billion were launched in the first three months of 1988.

Although precise figures aren't available, the global industry is thought to include about five hundred funds with total assets of $70 billion. In Canada, where an estimated thirty funds have about $2.5 billion in assets, closed-end funds haven't caught fire. But that doesn't mean they can't be useful, and profitable, alternatives to mutual funds for Canadian investors looking for diversification and professional management. Indeed, closed-end funds might be a better deal because they are out of favor.

Most Canadian funds usually trade at big discounts to net asset value. Discounts vary all over the map, but recently were in the twenty to twenty-five percent range. If the discount has narrowed by the time you sell your shares, you make money; if the discount has widened, you lose. To add to the attraction, dividends are paid one hundred cents on the dollar, even though you bought the fund at a discount.

No one realizes the comparative attractions of Canadian funds more than Thomas Herzfeld, a young Miami stockbroker and investment adviser who specializes in closed-end funds. For more than fifteen years Herzfeld has been making money trading U.S. closed-end funds and their British counterparts. A proponent of technical analysis, he uses arbitrage techniques similar to those used by commodity traders to try to catch the discounts at their highest and lowest points. He trades on movements as small as twelve cents.

Herzfeld made millions in the 1970s when U.S. closed-end funds traded, on average, at a twenty-five percent discount to net asset value. He made a killing when the spread in the United States narrowed to one or two percent during the early 1980s. Then he moved on to the more attractively priced British counterparts.

Since late 1986, however, he has been gobbling up shares in Canadian closed-end funds because of their discounts. He thinks they have a lot more room to rise than those in the United States and Britain. "If you're careful there are lots of good opportunities in closed-end funds," says Herzfeld, "and some of the best opportunities are in Canada."

Like mutuals, closed-end funds come in many forms. First to hit the market in Canada were the traditional, plain vanilla variety, for example Canadian General Investments and United Corporations Limited, which invest in straight equities.

Then the precious-metals funds hit the market in the early 1980s when gold prices soared to more than $430 an ounce. Unfortunately, soon after launch, the price of gold plummeted and these investments promptly lost value. But the funds benefited from the strong increase in gold prices in 1986 and 1987.

The recent bull market led to a proliferation of new closed-end funds. One of the hottest new concepts is foreign funds, many of which invest in a single city, country or geographical region. There are funds investing in Korea, Bangkok, India, Mexico, West Germany, Italy, Brazil, New Zealand, Scandinavia and Taiwan. Some, such as the Korea fund, represent the only way Canadians can buy stocks from a certain country. If stocks are too risky for your blood, there are other opportunities, such as the Global Government Plus Fund, launched in early 1988, which invests in government bonds from twenty-one countries.

Investment performance isn't the only consideration in buying one-country funds. These funds usually don't trade on Canadian exchanges. Although local brokers can buy a closed-end fund that trades in New York or London, chances are they don't follow those exchanges. Moreover, most Canadian newspapers don't publish fund prices, which means that following your investment is difficult. So you'll have to do your own research.

You'll probably also have to write overseas for a prospectus. Read it carefully to make sure all money raised goes into the market in which you're interested. And make sure the fund is diversified among industries and companies within a particular country or region, to give you greater protection.

Another kind of closed-end fund that is becoming increasingly popular is the "dual purpose" fund. These investments offer two classes of stock, one for people who prefer dividends and another for those who like capital gains.

The number of exotic closed-end funds is endless. You can buy funds that invest in currency futures, or shares of crown corporations being sold off by European governments. Then there is Guaranty Trust Company's Balanced Income and Growth Fund, which guarantees your initial invested income and therefore should prevent the shares from going to a discount. In 1988, Thomas Herzfeld was getting set to launch a Canadian-based fund that would invest in other closed-end funds traded around the globe.

The key to profiting from a closed-end fund is to buy when the discounts are wide and sell when the price moves closer to the net asset value. Discounts can shrink for two reasons.

Investor sentiment can become more positive; or the discount can be wiped out when a closed-end fund goes "open ended," or liquidates.

"Open ending" means investors who purchased shares at a discount can redeem them at their net asset value and reap big profits by capturing the entire discount. When a fund liquidates, shareholders receive net asset value less any expenses, while the manager loses its annual management fee. There are big profits for investors who purchased shares at a substantial discount; they can now redeem the shares at the net asset value per share.

Speculating on an open ending is big business in the United States, where most of the buying is done by pros like Thomas Herzfeld. Often, they acquire a large position in a fund, then solicit support from other investors to force management to open end the fund. Herzfeld has been involved in more than twenty reorganizations in the United States.

Open ending has been gaining adherents in Canada, where many early investors have grown tired of persistent discounts. Sparking most of the action has been Guardian Capital Incorporated, which "open ended" several of its closed-end funds during 1987 and early 1988.

But speculating on which funds might be candidates for open ending is tricky. Many fund managers have concentrated on bettering their performance in recent years, partly to ward off such a threat. Others buy back their own shares on the market to shrink the discount. And, of course, there is no guarantee that management will convert a closed-end fund to an open one and thus enable the investor to capture the entire discount.

Herzfeld and others don't recommend buying closed-end

funds only to make a big gain from an open ending. But they suggest taking a close look at the shareholder list before buying a fund. Should a proxy fight develop over reorganizing the fund, it helps to know who the larger shareholders are likely to side with.

Not everyone thinks small investors should consider closed-end funds. Critics argue that the only people who really make a killing are the managers. They have a stable pool of clients to deal with – unlike the managers of a mutual fund – and are paid a fixed management fee based on the size of the pool of investors' cash.

And investors can face some big risks. For example, the manager might not be able to deliver as good a performance as was achieved in the past. There is the risk of the portfolio and the possibility that investor sentiment will sag, pushing share prices even farther down.

If you want to buy closed-end funds, start by considering the same criteria you would use to pick any mutual fund. Examine historical performance to ensure that the fund is strong. Look closely at the fund's portfolio to make sure it meets your risk criteria. Because lack of sponsorship from the brokerage community can be a problem, you may have to dig hard to find information about the fund.

Monitoring the movement of discounts is a critical part of playing the closed-end fund market. Calculating the spread is easy: simply look at the fund's recent net asset value per share (NAVPS), which is published in the financial papers. Then slide your finger along to the list of stock quotes, and find the stock's latest share price. Calculate the difference between the market price and the NAVPS, divide by the NAVPS, multiply by a hundred and you've got your discount.

Herzfeld's rule of thumb is to buy closed-end fund shares

once the discount is five percent wider than its historical average. To be certain the shares are really bargains, you should make sure they are selling at steeper discounts than the discounts on similar funds.

You might also be well advised to avoid closed-end issues until they've been trading for a while. Many new issues trade around their net asset values in the first few months after issue, largely because the underwriters often buy heavily to support the market. Usually, though, the discount increases after three to six months.

Chapter 4

Mutual Funds as Registered Retirement Savings Plan Investments

THE AD FROM Trimark Investment Management Incorporated catches your eye. A no-nonsense, well-dressed young career woman stares straight out of the page. "I don't intend to work this hard all my life. That's why I switched to a Trimark RSP," the copy reads.

Early each year, newspapers and magazines are jammed with ads from mutual-fund management companies anxious to capture a chunk of the billions of dollars flowing into registered retirement savings plans. Although RRSP contributions can be made any time, taxpayers have sixty days after year-end to make RRSP contributions that will be tax-deductible for the previous year. Most people who contribute leave it to the last minute, so each January and February represent a big mutual-fund sales bonanza.

With RRSP contribution limits slated to increase in stages in the next several years, the amount of money being invested will grow rapidly. In 1988, if you don't belong to a company pension plan, you can put twenty percent of your earned income, or $7,500, whichever is less, into an RRSP. By 1990, you'll be able to salt away eighteen percent or $15,500. (Earned income is primarily wages and salaries.)

Mutual funds, of course, are just one of many investment options for your RRSP. Historically, the most popular have been term deposits and guaranteed investment certificates. But funds are becoming huge favorites, particularly as a result of the recent bull stock market. During the bull market, fund-management companies aggressively pushed the potential for capital gains available with equity funds.

But after the crash, fund marketing predictably took a different tack. Fund companies began emphasizing the safety and security of income funds. By most accounts, their strategy struck a responsive chord. Scorched by the crash, investors moved to conservative investments. Many probably moved out of mutual funds altogether, to guaranteed investments or term deposits.

Given the risk inherent in the stock market, what type of mutual funds should you put in your RRSP? Finding the answer to that involves understanding what an RRSP is, and carefully assessing how much risk you can tolerate, as well as knowing when you want to retire. The main goal of an RRSP is not to save you from paying taxes, as some advertisements seem to imply, but to build a pool of capital for retirement. If you plan to rely on your RRSP savings when you retire, you should consider adopting a fairly conservative approach to the type of investments you put in your plan. The federal government, in fact, won't allow you to invest your RRSP money in dicey propositions such as commodity-futures contracts. As equity funds are generally riskier than their fixed-income counterparts, perhaps stuffing your RRSP full of equity funds may not be such a brainy idea.

There are also tax factors to mull over if you consider investing your RRSP contribution in equity funds. Ottawa has provided some enormous incentives to invest in equities outside tax-sheltered arrangements such as RRSPs. For example, investments outside an RRSP are eligible for Ottawa's $100,000 lifetime capital-gains exemption. Any capital gains or losses realized inside a tax shelter, such as an RRSP, do not receive this favorable tax treatment. As well, the dividend tax credit, which effectively lowers the rate of tax on dividends, does not apply to dividends earned by stocks inside an RRSP. Note that your money is fully taxable when you eventually pull it out of your plan. Add this up, and you've got a reasonable case against putting equity funds in an RRSP.

But on the other hand, many people counter that if you avoid stocks or stock funds altogether, you're missing the possibility of greater long-term returns. After all, they say, the objective of an RRSP investment strategy is to create as large a pool of capital as you can before your retirement. Equities have provided historically better returns than guaranteed investments, such as term deposits.

A big factor that will help you settle on what type of funds to put in your plan is the amount of time you have before your planned retirement. It's not a particularly wise idea to assume the increased risk of a stock fund if you are only a few years away from receiving your company watch. If you do opt for risky stocks and take a beating in the market, you have precious few years to rebuild your capital pool. Younger investors can probably assume a greater degree of risk because they have sufficient time to recover if their stocks flop. You should consider investing in equity funds in your early years, but shift to more stable, fixed-income funds as you approach retirement.

Once you take a close look at the marketplace, you'll see that there are lots of RRSP-eligible funds available. To qualify, funds can invest no more than ten percent in foreign securities. When you scan our fund-performance tables, you'll note that those eligible for RRSPs are clearly flagged. To help, we've also made a list of the best performing RRSP-eligible funds for recent five- and ten-year periods.

The diversity of RRSP-eligible funds is a big plus. You can tailor a portfolio to suit your investment preferences. If you don't want a lot of risk, you can put money into bond and money-market funds. If you can tolerate more uncertainty, there are always those seductive equity funds. And if you invest in a mutual-fund family, you can manage your risk exposure. These families allow you to switch from one fund to another at little or no cost, which means you can capitalize on moves in the market.

Finding the most appropriate mix of funds is very much an individual exercise. Age, ability to tolerate risk and personal financial circumstances should be carefully considered. To help you in this exercise, we've asked a couple of financial planners, Kent McKelvey of Toronto-based Windcroft Financial Planning Limited and Tony De Thomasis of De Thomas Financial Corporation, to look at three imaginary investors.

Let's say you're twenty-five, have no major financial commitments and have $10,000 available for investment in your RRSP. With forty years to go to retirement, our experts say you should consider investing everything in equity funds. But remember, at age twenty-five you might still be planning a major purchase such as a house sometime in the future. You will want to have enough cash available for a down payment. Kent McKelvey suggests investing ten or twenty percent of your cash in a bond fund or a balanced fund. (A balanced fund invests in both stocks and bonds.) A bond fund is very liquid and provides a better return than bank-guaranteed investment certificates or term deposits, where your money is often locked in for a year or more. One possibility is the London Life Bond Fund, which in the past ten years has posted a twelve-percent average annual compound rate of return. There's also MacKenzie Mortgage and Income Fund, which has returned an average of thirteen percent annually over the same period. The rest of your $10,000, McKelvey says, should go into a well-run equity fund with a good long-term growth record, like Royfund Equity Fund.

Tony De Thomasis agrees that capital appreciation is a major objective. "You're probably hoping for maximum growth, and you shouldn't have to worry about getting money out early," he says. He recommends splitting the $10,000 between two high-quality equity funds, like Trimark Canadian Fund and AGF Growth Equity Fund. "These two are managed aggressively and should provide good long-term growth," he reports. An added bonus with AGF, a management company responsible for a family of funds, is that you can switch to another AGF fund at minimum cost, should the need arise.

The advice of our two planners doesn't change dramatically if you're forty and you have a family, a mortgage and $40,000 available in your plan. Both planners think that equity funds are the way to go, as you have lots of time before your retirement. McKelvey recommends funds with good long-term track records, such as Royfund Equity.

De Thomasis suggests taking ninety percent of your plan and buying into top-quality funds like Industrial Equity and Mackenzie Equity. To add a little spice to your portfolio, he also recommends funds that put money in foreign securities. Under federal law, you can invest up to ten percent of the book value of your plan in foreign securities. In the past several years, international equity funds have become quite popular, largely due to their sparkling performance. You can invest in country-specific funds, which buy shares of companies in one country, or global funds, which put money in operations in different countries. If investing in specific countries has little appeal, De Thomasis says a global fund or a fund that invests at least partly offshore may be the best bet. Templeton Growth Fund, run by venerable Templeton Management Incorporated, has one of the best long-term records.

Our pair of experts recommends a more dramatic shift in strategy as you approach retirement. Assume you're sixty-five, with the mortgage paid off and $75,000 to invest in your RRSP. McKelvey says preservation of capital should be a big concern. At the same time, he thinks you should be concerned about the effects of inflation on your retirement income. He suggests splitting your RRSP portfolio evenly between bond and equity funds. Bond funds will provide your plan with steady income, while the equity funds offer some protection from inflation.

De Thomasis's approach is slightly different. He recommends keeping one-third of your RRSP in bond or mortgage funds, which provide steady income as well as liquidity, particularly important if you need to cash a portion of your plan. Another third of your RRSP should go into a fund that spreads its investments among bonds, government of Canada treasury bills, Canadian stocks and foreign securities. One example is Dynamic Managed Portfolio. The remainder should be socked away into a high-quality Canadian equity fund. As De Thomasis says, "Your biggest fear is inflation, and the equity fund should provide an inflation hedge."

Chapter 5

Playing the Game

WHO SELLS MUTUAL FUNDS? These days, a better question might be, who doesn't? With mutual funds clearly one of Canadians' most popular investments, everyone is getting into the sales game. Historically, the biggest sellers of mutual funds have been independent fund dealers who handle a variety of investment products and tax shelters but depend upon mutual funds for most of their revenues. The Investment Funds Institute of Canada (IFIC) reports that there are now 2,100 fund specialists registered in Canada. Canada's largest independent dealer is Regal Capital Planners Limited, with almost three hundred salespeople across Canada. In Ontario alone, the number of independent brokers has grown from ten firms to fifty since 1983. In the midwest, Pro-Fund distributors is the biggest. In British Columbia, Great Pacific Management Company, which has more than one hundred and eighty sales agents, dominates the business.

In the past few years, the big sales push has come from the

eleven thousand stockbrokers across Canada. After years of thinking of funds as a minor sideline to stocks and bonds, brokerage houses are now aggressively pushing funds. And they're securing a big piece of the pie in the process. Brokers, in fact, now account for more than half of Canadian mutual-fund sales. So important are fund commissions to brokerage-house profitability that there's hardly a firm that doesn't have its own mutual-fund marketing department.

Some fund-management companies sell their funds directly to investors. Some fund organizations also market their funds without a sales fee, and also sell directly to investors.

Mutual funds sponsored by trust companies and banks can be bought through their extensive branch networks. Life-insurance companies also sell their funds directly to clients, although you generally have to be a policy owner to participate. IFIC reports that there are nearly three thousand life-insurance agents who are also registered to sell mutual funds.

If you're confused by this proliferation of salespeople, you've got lots of company. But there's a positive side to the competition – that is, if you're willing to shop around for the best deal. There's usually plenty of room for fee negotiation. As you shop among sales agents, pick the one who provides the best service.

No matter who they work for, all sales agents have passed the educational courses required by the Investment Funds Institute of Canada or the Canadian Securities Institute; all are registered with the relevant securities commissions.

What are salespeople responsible for?

- They must explain the fund's objectives and terms in language that is understandable to new, often unsophisticated investors.

- They must handle client inquiries about contractual and withdrawal plans, dividend payments, transfer privileges and other features of the fund.
- They must accept and transmit orders for fund share redemptions.
- They must mail out confirmations of sales.

When you are meeting a sales agent, ask plenty of questions, including how the agent is compensated. Note that some agents are offered exotic trips and lavish prizes, which may blur their objectivity. The Investment Dealer's Association, which governs stockbrokers, is considering clamping down on this practice.

How much is all the diversification and professional management of mutual funds going to cost you? Probably more than you think. Mutual-fund organizations are constantly devising new ways to hit you with charges – and new ways to disguise those charges.

The brokers and dealers who sell the funds argue that fees become meaningless if the funds chalk up superior long-term performance. That's a big if. Fees do reduce the yield on funds, especially if you invest for a short time. Let's say you invest in a fund with a nine-percent annual sales fee and a two-percent annual management fee. Your fund has to increase in value by eleven percent in the first year for you to stay even.

Fees vary sharply from fund to fund. How much you pay will depend, among other things, upon your investment savvy, how much you're investing and how good a negotiator you are. Take heart: the fees and charges are not as baffling as they seem.

"Load" or sales fee

A "load" is an acquisition charge, and the amount is clearly stated in the prospectus of each mutual fund. When you pay this fee, you are absorbing the fund organization's cost of marketing.

Most fund organizations don't have their own salespeople, and they rely on commission-driven brokers and agents for sales. Often more than seventy-five percent of the acquisition fee goes to the broker or sales agents.

But there's room for limited maneuvering on your part. Although the load can be as high as nine percent of the amount you invest, discounting is widespread, and only a few funds insist on the full levy. Generally, if you buy from a full-service stockbroker, four or five percent is the norm. And if you have more than $10,000 to invest, you can usually swing a better deal. The lowest fees are usually available from discount brokers, such as Marathon Brown and Company or the Toronto Dominion Bank's Green Line Investors Service, whose commissions are half those of full-service stockbrokers, and much less than those of many mutual-funds salespeople.

The load comes off the top, which means you have less money working for you than you thought. For instance, if you invest $10,000 in the Templeton Growth Fund, which charges 8.5%, you'd have only $9,150 invested in fund units.

The sales fee gets smaller as the amount you are investing increases. Here, for instance, is how it works with Templeton Growth Fund:

Sale amount	**Commission**
Less than $12,000	8.50%
$12,000 but less than $30,000	7.75%

$30,000 but less than $60,000	6.25%
$60,000 but less than $120,000	4.50%
$120,000 but less than $300,000	2.75%
$300,000 but less than $1.2 million	1.50%
$1.2 million but less than $2.4 million	0.75%
$2.4 million or more	0.50%

Management fees

This fee is the price you pay for that professional portfolio management, which fund organizations are so fond of talking about. You don't pay it directly; it is deducted monthly from the assets of the fund, usually at the rate of one to two percent of assets under administration and is levied annually. That means that as your fund assets grow, so do the fees, and the fund manager walks away with more of your money.

A comparison of management fees doesn't tell you how much you're forking over to the fund company. Many mutual funds have administration costs that aren't included in management fees. These costs also come out of the fund's assets – in other words, they are paid by the shareholders. These additional administrative costs include printing and mailing, legal fees, auditing, office overhead and brokerage fees for trading securities.

To get an idea of how much you would pay for the running of the different funds, you could compare "expense ratios." The expense ratio is the sum of the management fees and administrative costs expressed as a percentage of the total annual assets of a fund. The expense-ratio figure isn't always available in the prospectus, but it is contained in the fund's annual financial statement and in the annual information form that's filed with provincial securities regulators.

Small funds tend to have relatively greater expenses because there are fewer assets over which to spread the costs. As they grow, the expense ratios theoretically should decline. One notable example is the huge Templeton Growth Fund, which has an extremely low expense ratio of less than one percent.

During the past few years, some fund companies have used the sales boom to hike their expense and management charges. They claim their basic costs have increased significantly because of the large numbers of new unit holders.

Generally, expense ratios for Canadian equity funds average two percent; some funds charge half a percent more or less. Over time, a higher expense ratio will cost you big bucks. But you shouldn't let a higher expense ratio turn you off a superior fund. The important factor to consider is how the ratio compares to performance numbers. Return figures are reported after expenses. So if a fund really makes money for you, the expense ratio matters little. The better the performance record of the fund, the less you should concern yourself with the fee.

Some companies have started splitting management fees with brokers and other salespeople as an incentive to push their funds. Fund organizations justify these "trailing commissions," also known as "service fees," by claiming they are intended to compensate brokers for continuing client advice and service. Whether you get what you pay for is another question altogether.

12b-1 plans

In one relatively new management-fee wrinkle, fund management dips into its own fund assets to pay marketing costs. This wrinkle gets its name from U.S. Securities and Exchange Commission Rule 12b-1, which first allowed the paying of costs with assets in the United States.

These funds don't charge front-end acquisition fees, but they still provide the sales agents with an up-front commission. What makes these funds different from more traditional funds is that the fund management company itself puts up the commission. The fund then takes a chunk of the annual management fees to cover distribution costs.

But that doesn't mean you escape paying some of the marketing costs. The fund organization usually beefs up the management fee to recover its out-of-pocket expenses on the front-end commission paid to the broker. What's more, there's almost always a sliding-scale "back-end load" – an amount charged against the higher value of your investment when you sell your units. MacKenzie Financial Corporation's Industrial Horizon Fund, for example, one of the first of the 12b-1 funds in Canada, pays the broker four-percent commission, then recoups its costs through a cut of the annual management fee. It also charges a back-end load, which drops from four percent to nothing in nine years. This fee will discourage you from cashing out early to try to avoid paying the marketing costs.

Transfer fees

These can be important if you plan to shuffle your assets as market conditions and your investment goals change. Some companies allow switching between funds in the same group for free, while others charge a flat rate for each move, usually $15 to $20, or a maximum of two percent of the assets under management.

RRSP fees

Mutual funds held in registered retirement savings plans (RRSPs) could face an annual trustee levy, usually a minimum of $15. If you want to have mutual funds from different companies in your plan, you have to set up RRSP accounts with each company and pay each company a separate fee. The alternative is a self-directed RRSP, which holds all your mutual funds under a single trust arrangement. The trustee – in fact, a trust company – may charge its own withdrawal fee when the plan is closed.

Service fees

These are usually charged on money-market funds to pay the management company for making daily calculations of accrued interest on units. These service fees are comparatively low.

When you buy or redeem your shares, you do so at a price equal to the fund's net asset value per share. This is the theoretical amount a fund's shareholders would receive for each share if the fund were to sell all its portfolio of investments at market value, collect all receivables, pay all liabilities and distribute what is left to shareholders.

Expressed as a simple formula: net asset value per share equals total assets (including portfolio at market price) minus total liabilities divided by the total number of units.

Making the buy is easy. If you have the cash, the simplest way to start is to make a single payment and buy as many shares as you can afford. Usually, $500 to $1,000 is the minimum investment. With cash purchases, you can buy as many shares as you want. It's even possible to buy fractions of shares. If, for instance, you invest $550 in a fund that has an offering price of $4 per share, you will receive, excluding sales charges, 137½ shares ($550 divided by $4).

If you can't make a large initial outlay, you might want to try some kind of dollar-cost averaging plan, which involves investing a fixed amount of money regularly. That means you'll be able to buy more units when prices decrease and fewer when they increase.

The plan can be voluntary or contractual. With a voluntary plan, you agree to set aside a minimum sum of money from a bank or trust-company account at regular intervals. The amount can be increased or decreased at any time at your discretion. Investors in voluntary accumulation plans can discontinue payments to the plan at any time without penalty and can redeem their shares at any time.

Under a contractual plan, you agree to buy stipulated dollar amounts at specified periods over a predetermined number of years. With this arrangement, you pay the sales commission for the whole transaction in one lump sum when the deal is struck. As a result, there's a heavy penalty if you decide to discontinue the plan before its expiry date. (See Chapter Six)

Many funds will automatically reinvest dividends into new shares of the fund at the prevailing net asset value without a sales charge on shares so purchased.

If you're buying a load fund, your broker or financial planner has to furnish you with a fund prospectus and recent financial statements so you can be sure the fund's and your objectives coincide. You must also provide all the information required by provincial securities commissions – name, address, age, name of spouse and investment objectives – to help ensure that the fund is suitable for you. (Sales agents call this the "know your client" rule.) Suitability standards are as important in mutual-fund sales as they are in the general securities business.

Then the dealer telephones the order to a central mutual-fund clearing house or to the fund management company. As long as the order is made before 4:00 P.M., you'll receive the fund's net asset value per share on the day of the transaction.

Usually, you'll get a record of the transaction from your dealer, including the number of units purchased and the net asset value on the day you enter the order. A confirmation slip from the fund management company should come in the mail within a month.

Independent dealers usually require that you pay up front. But you've got a week to pay a stockbroker for the purchase, even though brokers buy the fund units themselves for resale and are technically on the hook for the fund units once they place your order.

If you decide to register your units in your own name, confirmation of the purchase from the fund management company is usually all you'll need by way of registration. If you're the type of person who likes to physically hold your investments, make sure you tuck them away in a safety deposit box or safe; losing your certificates can cost you four percent of the value of your units upon redemption.

Stockbrokers usually urge you to register your funds in their firm's name. That makes it easier when it comes to cashing out, since the broker can redeem the units directly. But it causes new problems, as all information from the fund organization will go to the firm instead of to you. That means you've got to depend on the broker to pass along the important information. Or you can give the fund organization your name and address, and ask them to send you information. Securities regulators are now working on a system whereby important information is sent to nonregistered securities holders.

Every time you buy or redeem units registered in your name or receive a dividend or capital-gains distribution, you'll receive a confirmation slip. Keep those – you'll need them when tax time comes around.

And that's not all you should expect from the fund manager. Each January you will also receive a statement of records from the fund management company with a complete summary of all transactions that took place in your account, including total dividends and capital gains paid out during the past year.

You will also receive quarterly, semiannual and annual reports. These usually include a letter from the fund president or manager saying wonderful things about the fund's performance. Then there will be a lot of statistics about performance and the change in assets. There will also be a list of the securities the fund now holds, generally broken down into bonds, stocks, cash and "other."

By law, mutual-fund corporations (as opposed to mutual fund trusts) must hold a meeting of shareholders once each year. Usually the meeting coincides with the board of directors meeting, which means that the directors will be there along with management representatives. That's a good time to ask any questions about the fund's operation.

Getting out is harder than getting in – especially if the fund units are registered in your name. If the units are in your broker's name, notify your broker, who takes care of it for you. If you are the registered owner, you'll have trouble redeeming any fund account worth more than $10,000 unless your signature is guaranteed by a broker, bank or trust company. Once you succeed in getting out, you get the net asset value on the day the request is filed with the fund management company. The fund operator has seven days to send you your cash. Almost all funds reserve the right to suspend or defer a shareholder's privilege to redeem his or her shares, but that right is used only in extremely rare circumstances, such as if the stock exchange suspends trading.

One of the best ways to get your money out of a mutual fund is through systematic withdrawal plans, which allow you to retrieve all or part of the capital you invested, plus dividends, over a period of time. If the fund portfolio increases in value, the increased worth of the fund's shares helps to offset the reduction of principal that results from the planned withdrawal. But the investor's capital will shrink if the net asset value of the fund does not increase by more than the amount of the withdrawal.

There are several systematic withdrawal plans.

- Ratio Withdrawal Plan. Each year, you submit a certain

percentage of your fund shares for redemption. Naturally, the higher the percentage, the more rapid the rate of depletion of your original investment.

• Fixed Dollar Withdrawal Plan. Here you choose the specified dollar amount you wish to withdraw regularly.

• Fixed Period Withdrawal Plan. In this plan, a specified amount of capital and dividends is withdrawn over a determined period of time; all capital will be exhausted when the plan ends.

• Annuity. Life annuities guarantee an income to buyers for as long as they live, and may be offered only by government-certified annuity issuers. Some mutual funds collaborate with life-insurance companies to offer such plans. Payments are made out of your original capital plus interest and other income earned on the capital. Normally, life annuity payments cease when you die, even if you haven't recouped your original investment. If you live a long life, you receive more than you invested. If you die young, you don't get as much.

Securities regulators have had their hands full keeping up with the growth in the mutual-funds industry. The huge jump in the number of funds in Canada – and the number of men and women selling them – has left provincial regulatory bodies like the Ontario Securities Commission struggling with many thorny administrative problems.

Generally, mutual-fund managers, distributors and their sales personnel must all be registered with the securities commissions in which they operate. But there are other restrictions in place. Usually, fund managers can't:

• purchase more than ten percent of the total securities of a single issuer

• purchase a control position in a company

- buy stock on margin or "sell short" (sell securities they don't own, hoping to buy them back more cheaply later on)
- buy commodity futures contracts
- buy unlisted stocks, real estate or illiquid securities sold through private placement.

Sales agents' ethics may be occasionally compromised in the chase for big commission dollars. Performance figures are one sore point: some outfits advertise superior short-term performance figures in the eighty to ninety percent range to catch an investor's eye. As well, some funds promise exotic trips and prizes, to lure brokers and sales agents into peddling a particular fund. (This practice may soon be restricted.)

Sales incentives, of course, are common in many industries. The difference here is that agents pass themselves off as impartial advisors. They don't always say they have an incentive to sell a particular fund.

In November 1987, the Ontario Securities Commission (OSC) brought down a comprehensive set of mutual-fund rules, which dealt extensively with advertising. Companies are no longer able to compare the performance of their fund to other funds, or to a bench-mark index, such as the Toronto Stock Exchange 300 Composite Index. Radio advertising is not allowed. Any literature showing a fund's past compound annual growth rate must carry a warning, in the same size print, that numbers "are used only for the purpose of illustrating the effects of compound growth rates and do not purport to forecast future returns." The new OSC rules also require funds to plainly state all compensation paid to brokers in the fund prospectus. It is up to you to read the document.

Sales literature must indicate the fund's long-term record over one, three and five years, and not state just how it has performed during a particularly hot short-term period. Tables showing the potential effect of compound rates of return must clearly state that there is no guarantee of future fund values or returns. And any reference to a rate-of-return figure must note that the figure is reduced by the amount of any sales charges, redemption fees or other fees or expenses that are payable by the investor.

The Investment Funds Institute of Canada frowns on a number of sales practices. These include

- Selling other investments to buy mutual funds, unless it can be clearly shown that the sale is in the client's best interest and that the client is aware of the charges involved.
- Unnecessary switching from fund to fund, particularly if fees are involved.
- Recommending the borrowing of money for purchases.
- Buying on margin.
- Overemphasizing the immediate tax savings available through an RRSP.

Agent sales licenses are renewed annually, and may be revoked at any time, which means that regulators can easily revoke a license if an agent isn't playing by the rules.

Fund distributors are prohibited from "co-mingling" fund assets. That means that money earmarked for mutual funds can't be used by the fund company for anything other than buying securities, paying redemptions or paying service fees to which the principal distributor is entitled. The distributor has to keep fund money in an interest-bearing trust account.

Funds and taxes

Picking out winners among the hundreds of mutual funds is difficult enough – and you also have to satisfy the folks at Revenue Canada. Keeping them happy may not be a pleasant or easy task, as Canada's tax system has become so complex that even the experts have difficulty figuring it out. One of the latest complications is the federal government's ambitious tax reform package, introduced in 1985 and substantially amended in 1987. The reforms could mean that more of your investment dollars land in Ottawa's pocket. In its zeal to close loopholes and make the tax system more equitable, the federal government has reduced – in some cases significantly – some tax benefits.

The thinking behind the taxation of mutual funds is that funds represent conduits for the income and capital gains that flow from the individual securities the fund buys and sells. The idea is that, at the end of the day, fund investors should be in the same general tax position they would be in if they invested directly in the securities held by the fund. There are two main tax areas to consider. One is the treatment of capital gains, the amount by which the selling price of a security exceeds its original purchase price. The other is how Revenue Canada gets its due from dividends, the regular earnings your fund produces. Here are some general observations about the tax treatment of funds. Remember that the comments correspond to rules that were in effect when our book was written. Reforms will inevitably change the picture, so you should check carefully with your accountant when you're thinking about taxes and how they affect your investment strategy.

Mutual funds can operate as trusts or as corporations.

Because mutual-fund trusts don't pay any taxes, they are by far the most common types. When you invest in a mutual-fund trust, you buy units; when you invest in a corporation, you buy shares. But whether you invest in a corporation or a trust won't make a whole lot of difference to your daily investment activities. In fact, most investors, even sophisticated ones, don't know what type of fund they bought. But it is an important distinction to consider at tax time.

Before the 1985 reform, the taxation of capital gains was fairly straightforward: half of any capital gain was taxable. (The amount of the gain on which you pay tax is called the taxable capital gain.) In 1985, Ottawa introduced the $500,000 lifetime capital-gains exemption for Canadian residents. This allowed you to earn, tax-free, up to $500,000 of capital gains ($250,000 taxable capital gains) in your lifetime. The exemption was cumulative and was to be phased in over five years, eventually reaching the $500,000 limit in 1990.

However, in the 1987 budget, Ottawa took a broad swipe at the exemption, reducing its attractiveness in several ways. First, Ottawa froze the lifetime limit at $100,000 ($50,000 taxable capital gains) for most types of capital gains. Second, the federal government boosted the amount of gain you have to include in your income for tax purposes (called the inclusion rate). This rate increased to 66.67% in 1988, from 50% in previous years, and will move to 75% in 1990.

But Ottawa also wanted to hit those investors who "double dip." Before 1987, investors could deduct the interest costs of any money they borrowed to make an investment. Then they could use the capital-gains exemption when the investment was sold. After 1987, the capital-gains exemption applies only to income that exceeds investment losses. These losses are defined as the amount by which your investment expense – including investment loan costs – exceeds your investment income. If you borrow to buy mutual-fund units, your access to the exemption will be severely curtailed.

With mutual funds, you can realize a capital gain in two ways. You might return your units to the fund for more than you paid, or you might receive a special distribution because of gains made by the fund. Let's say you earn the gains the first way, by redeeming for $500 the mutual-fund units that you bought last year for $100. That means your potential capital gain is $400.

Under 1987 rules, your taxable capital gain would be $200 (or half the $400 capital gain), and the full $200 was eligible for the exemption. But in 1988 and 1989, the portion of your capital that is taxable rises to $267 (or 66.67% of $400) as the inclusion rate increases; in 1990, it will be $300 (or 75% of $400). If you have already used your exemption, you'll likely have to pay more tax on the gains.

To add another wrinkle, let's assume you borrowed the $100 to buy your units, and that your interest expense over the year is $12. Let's also assume you earned no dividends from your investment during the year. That leaves you with an investment loss of $12. So the amount that could be sheltered in 1988 by the capital-gains exemption is $255 ($267 minus $12 in interest costs). Obviously, that's less than the $267 that you'd be able to shelter if you didn't take out a loan to buy your fund portfolio.

The payments you receive regularly from your fund are called dividends. But what the fund is actually passing along to you is a combination of dividend and other investment income, interest, for instance, earned on the securities the fund holds. How you treat your dividends from the fund depends on whether the fund is a corporation or a trust.

Dividends paid by Canadian mutual-fund corporations are treated the same as dividends paid by domestic companies. That's good news, because you pay less tax on dividends from Canadian companies than you would on interest income.

This tax benefit comes your way in the form of the dividend gross-up and credit system. Dividends are paid out of the corporation's after-tax income. Here's how the system works. The fund company will send you a T-4 slip outlining your dividend income. Then you "gross up" (or increase) the amount of dividends you receive by 25%. Then you apply, against your federal tax, a credit equal to 13.5% of the increased amount. The net effect of all this figuring is a lower rate of tax than you would otherwise pay. If you live in Ontario in 1988 and pay tax at the top rate of 43.5%, you'll pay only 30% on dividends.

If you have units of a mutual-fund trust, the situation is slightly different. Unlike a corporation, a trust does not pay tax. It sends you a T-3 slip, which breaks down interest and dividend income. You'll be able to take advantage of the dividend gross-up and credit system for the dividend portion. But the interest portion receives no such favorable treatment, and you'll have to pay tax on it as you would on interest income from any other source. You might think that if you invest in a mutual-fund trust, you will be worse off, from a tax standpoint, than if you invest in a corporation. But that's not true. In the case of the corporation, the dividends you receive have already been taxed at the corporate level. As a result, the dividend that flows to investors from a mutual-fund corporation would probably be less than the payments that flow from a mutual-fund trust.

If you have units in global funds that invest in securities in different foreign countries, you may be concerned about possible international tax complications. There's no difficulty with capital gains. You simply report them the same way you would with, say, a Canadian equity fund. Dividend income is another story. Because it flows more or less directly to you from the foreign company, you should be able to claim a foreign tax credit for the income received.

Chapter
6

Picking the Right Fund

UNDERSTANDING FUNDS IS ONE THING, but actually choosing the right fund is another. How will you, who needed a book to tell you about mutual funds, evaluate the suitability of one fund over another? How do you sort through the slick ad campaigns and heavyhanded sales pitches used to market funds these days?

Simple: do your homework. Don't depend on a financial planner or broker to put you in the right fund; you should make your own investment decisions. No one is going to care as much about your money as you do. And no one but you will manage it for free.

When you consider buying a mutual fund, remember that sales agents have their own motives; after all, they make a living from the commissions they earn. So don't be surprised if you hear lots from salespeople about funds that, as it turns out, offer exotic trips and prizes to reward big sellers.

With the help of our performance tables, at the back of the book, you can probably do just as well as the average broker or financial planner in picking the right mutual fund. Although there's no easy formula to help you find the fund that's appropriate for you, there are some basic questions to ask when shopping around.

First, what are your financial goals? Why you are investing? A surprising number of people can't answer this basic question. But it is the starting point for picking a fund.

Do you want to put your kid through college, take a trip around the world or buy a Florida condominium when you retire? Are you looking for a big capital gain, steady income or a tax break?

Mapping out a plan is the key to financial independence. After you clearly define your personal objectives and the time in which you want to achieve them, it will be easier to pick the most appropriate type of fund.

As well, you should ask yourself how much risk you can handle. It is critical to select funds that reflect your ability to withstand risk. And your risk quotient depends on everything from your psychological makeup – you have to be able to sleep at night – to the amount of time left before you retire.

If, for instance, you're near retirement and will soon need a steady income, a bond fund that invests in quality corporate and government bonds could be appealing. On the other hand, if you're looking for rapid capital growth to meet, say, a child's college tuition in a few years, you might opt for an aggressive growth fund or a sector fund that has potential for big gains.

Knowing which type of fund is suitable isn't enough. Keep in mind that, while all mutual funds are diversified, some spread the risks more widely than others. A Canadian equity fund, for instance, will own shares in a wider range of industries than a precious-metals fund. Remember, also, that your need for diversification will probably increase as your personal assets grow.

The risk inherent in a fund isn't always apparent. A fund can rack up hefty long-term performance gains, but that doesn't count for much if it slumps just before you want to cash out. That's where our mutual fund tables can help. Look at the column called "variability." That refers to the degree to which the monthly rate of return fluctuates. (We give you one figure for the whole year.)

For instance, our tables show us that Cundill Security Fund gained an average of 13.8% annually and United Accumulative Retirement Fund gained an average of 13.9% annually during the past five years. But the tables show that United Accumulative, which received a below average variability ranking (indicated as "avg –" in our table), gave shareholders less of a buffeting than the average Canadian equity fund. The Cundill fund, on the other hand, was more volatile and received a ranking of above average ("avg +"). That means you had a greater chance of cashing out at a loss with the Cundill fund.

Appraising volatility is particularly difficult if a fund doesn't have an established track record. Take a good look at a new fund's prospectus, to be sure that its goals match your own.

Now you have to look at how the funds perform. That's more complicated than it sounds. You might snap up the funds with the best one-year record, but that may be suicide. Last year's results are no indicator of this year's. Indeed, last year's winner could well be this year's loser.

You should look for an "all-weather fund" – one that has a history of doing respectably in both bull and bear markets.

Consistency is everything. During the 1988 bull market, plenty of funds posted enticing gains. But too often investors stock up on the fastest-rising funds just as the market and the funds are running out of steam. Likewise, after a long slump, too many investors cling to the most conservative funds at exactly the wrong time.

Look for funds that have stood the test of time. Performance should be scrutinized for five to ten years; short-term numbers are deceiving. The good five- or ten-year track record ensures that the fund has performed well through entire market cycles. And remember that performance can fluctuate dramatically within short periods. If you buy into a fund and stay with it for a few years, the fund manager has time to weather market downturns and to profit during the good times. (The tables at the back of the book rank fund performance for you.) Annual compound rate of return – the change in net asset value assuming all dividends and capital gains are reinvested – provides an appropriate measure that can be compared to returns on other investments and market bench marks, like the TSE 300 Composite Index, which measures the performance of three hundred of the better-known stocks listed on the Toronto Stock Exchange. To make your job easier, we've pulled out the best-performing funds for the five- and ten-year periods ended March 31, 1988 in various categories.

During that ten year period, Japanese stock funds have been the best around, turning in an average gain of 22.6% annually, most of it coming in the past five years. Equity funds, which invested mainly in Canada, gained an average of only 13.8% annually, compared to 16.5% by the Toronto Stock Exchange's Total Returns Index. (This reflects the performance of the TSE three hundred companies, assuming that dividends are reinvested.) Fixed income funds, on the other hand, gained 11%. This is less than the 12.6% gain by ScotiaMcleod's bench-mark long-corporate bond index during that period.

The performance figures you should weigh most heavily are those that correspond to the number of years you anticipate holding the investment. The idea is to compare similar funds, as well as to keep an eye on other comparable investments. But beware – the numbers can sometimes be deceiving. Foreign funds, for instance, can benefit from an appreciating currency but probably won't perform as strongly when the currency kick disappears.

All mutual funds involve a certain risk, but some funds make their risks pay off better than others. The risk may be worth it if a fund offers potentially high rewards. Therefore, you should slide your finger over to the column in our tables labeled "reward-risk ratio." The ratio is calculated by dividing the fund's compound rate of return by its variability. By itself, the figure is meaningless. But if you make comparisons among the different mutual funds and with market bench marks such as the TSE 300's total returns index, you should be able to identify which funds are best at making risks pay off.

For example, as the tables show, Associate Investors Fund's performance was extremely consistent for the five years ending March 31, 1988. But it gained an average of just 12% annually during that period and its reward-risk ratio was .27%. You would have had a rather low return for your risk. On the other hand, Bolton Tremblay International Fund gained 15% annually during the same period. However, it had a below-average return relative to its above-average volatility. Its ratio was .19%. One fund that really made its risks pay off was Cundill Value Fund, which gained an average of 14.9% annually, with average variability. Its reward-risk ratio was a healthy .41%.

Another point to remember is that the hefty sales commissions and other charges you pay help to determine how much cash you actually make.

The first question is whether you should pay a sales commission, or "load." Perhaps not. The brokers and dealers who charge these commissions argue that any commission you pay will seem small if the fund chalks up a superior long-term performance. But our calculations show that a number of no-load funds have proven to be better investments over five and ten years than their commission-charging counterparts, once you factor in the sales charges.

Our research confirms a mutual-fund adage: the longer you're in a successful fund, the less the sales charge matters. Hence, investors who intend to stay in for five years or less should cast a wary eye at load funds, unless the performance of the load fund is far superior to the performance of the no-load alternatives.

Brokers and sales agents contend that they more than compensate for sales charges through such services as portfolio analysis and personal attention. Realistically, though, service varies from agent to agent.

You should also have a close look at management fees, service charges and the other costs. (We discussed these in Chapter Four.) Our tables in the back of the book will indicate the operating costs for various funds.

Just as thoroughbred racing fans pour over names in the *Racing Form*, you should pay careful attention to the names and track records of the fund managers. Last week's winning horse can trail the pack this week if there's a different jockey in the saddle. Our performance scorecard makes it easy for you to follow the comings and goings of portfolio managers.

Many of the funds that perform best over long periods have had a single manager plotting strategy. For example, Martin Siegerman has been piloting Royfund Equity Fund for the past fifteen years. Peter Cundill has been running Cundill Value Fund, another steady performer, since its inception in 1979. And John Templeton has piloted the Templeton Growth Fund since 1954.

Knowing who the portfolio managers are – and how long they've been there – should be part of any investor's standard check list. Historical performance can be irrelevant if it was accomplished under a different manager than the one in charge today. Likewise, a long-time laggard can sparkle with a respected new manager.

Some mutual-fund organizations make it difficult to keep track of the lineup. Naturally, companies attracting well-regarded stock pickers trumpet their acquisitions. But fund companies aren't stupid; when they lose a star manager they keep it as quiet as possible.

Bolton Tremblay Funds Incorporated certainly didn't make a big noise when Robert Krembil quit running its Taurus Fund in 1981; he took two key employees with him and set up his own mutual-fund management team. The fund has stumbled since Krembil's exit. When well-regarded Peter Spark left Guaranty Trust Company of Canada in the fall of 1985 to join Bolton Tremblay, Bolton treated the move like the Second Coming.

You'll have to do your own research on this matter. Although a change of managers can clearly affect performance, fund-management companies are not required to disclose the identity of their stock pickers. They have to inform investors when there is a "material change" involving the fund, but it isn't always clear that a fund manager's defection qualifies as a material change. The Ontario Securities Commission examines management changes case by case. Normally, changes don't have to be reported unless they involve somebody of the importance of John Templeton.

Achieving consistent returns should be the most important goal in fund investing, but you should also decide how much liquidity you want from a fund. Some investors require instant access to their money, something that isn't available through all funds. Although most equity funds value their assets daily, others do it weekly or even monthly. A fund that values assets monthly will take longer to pay your money than one that values daily. And, while the fund has your money, how much control do you want over your own investment? Will you want to move your cash around as market conditions change or as your investment objectives change? If so, you'd probably be better off in a mutual fund "family," which allows you to transfer your money from fund to fund, usually without paying sales commissions. Compare the different fund "stables" run by Investors Group and AGF Management. As well, institutions like Royal Trust manage a wide swath of funds. Make sure that there are enough fund options to meet your various investment needs.

You should also find out how stable the fund organization is. The failure of one large organization, the Principal Group, in 1987, got many people worried about the financial stability of their fund organization. Before they can set up shop, mutual-fund companies are required to have a minimum amount of seed capital, and they must meet other strict financial criteria. Investors have additional protection because acounts and assets are in the hands of an independent financial organization, usually a trust company, that is appointed as the fund's custodian. Accounts and assets can't be touched by the management company under any circumstances. The custodian collects money received from investors and arranges for cash payouts through dividend payments, portfolio purchases and share redemptions.

One of the best ways to start your fund prospecting is to request prospectuses of the funds that catch your interest. By law, you must receive a prospectus before investing. Unfortunately, most investors ignore these fat legal documents. That's a mistake; there's some good information to be gleaned from prospectuses which contain information that funds are, by law, required to publish.

You should go over the documents with a magnifying glass; scour the fine print and footnotes.

The prospectus will contain a description of the fund's investment restrictions, policies and risk factors. Usually fund goals are something like: "Achieving capital appreciation over the longer term consistent with preservation of invested capital." Or: "To achieve strong growth of capital with a high degree of reliability over the long run." Such passages don't tell you much about how the fund is run. But they should give you a general idea about whether the fund meets your risk criteria.

There will also be details about fees, charges and expenses. Note which charges are paid by the fund manager and the mutual fund organization, and which charges you end up paying. Sales and redemption fees are clearly detailed. Ongoing expenses and other costs born by investors must be presented in table form and expressed in the expense ratio, which measures how much you pay toward the fund's annual upkeep and administration.

Incentives used by the funds to reward sales agents will be

listed. These incentives could blur agents' objectivity, and must be declared. This can make for interesting reading. Consider an early prospectus for Mackenzie Financial's Industrial Horizon Fund, which was launched in early 1987. It describes an annual conference, Mackenzie's major sales incentive program. "The entire cost of the Mackenzie Conference, including all travelling and accommodation expenses of attendees, is paid by Mackenzie, primarily from the portion of the selling commission which it retains on the sales of units and shares of its other sponsored mutual funds." By selling $175,000 worth of new Mackenzie fund units, a sales agent qualifies for the first three days of the conference in Dallas; $250,000 in sales gets an agent to a conference in Rome; if agents sell $850,000, they earn a cash bonus of $100 for each additional $10,000 in sales.

The prospectus will also include additional investment services offered. These services, which can include telephone redemptions and sales and withdrawal programs, are usually explained but shouldn't be a critical factor in your decision.

Chapter

7

Choosing the Right Strategy

THERE'S MORE TO MAKING MONEY in mutual funds than simply buying a fund and leaving the important decisions to a manager and a sales agent. You need self-discipline and investment smarts to profit. You also need a sensible investment plan, one that will allow you to glean the best possible returns in a good market and insulate you when the market turns sour. Your approach will depend upon your age, your income, your ability to withstand risk and your tax situation – all the things we talked about in Chapter Six, before you chose a fund. Now we have to take a long-term look at your investment. Unless you're one of those rare individuals who knows the precise times to buy and sell, the surest way to make money from funds is to buy for the long haul. Even a well-run fund won't produce much growth for a new investor in the first couple of years. Imagine you're investing $10,000. A five-percent up-front sales charge, the average these days, reduces the amount actually going into the fund to $9,500. The annual management fee, say two percent, will cost you $190. (This fee is not paid up front, but is deducted annually from fund assets.) The fund must grow by more than seven percent in the first year just to bring the value of your holdings back to $10,000.

Stock markets move in fairly regular cycles, so sooner or later everyone is out of step with the market. Having your money for a few years allows the fund manager to weather market downturns and to profit during the good times. Although there may be occasions when it pays to deviate from this course, most investment pros say you should leave your fund investments intact for at least three to five years, and preferably for ten to fifteen years.

That doesn't mean you should park your money and forget about it. It is important to closely monitor a fund and be ready to liquidate if its performance consistently lags behind the earnings of others of its type. You may conclude that the manager simply isn't going to come through, and that you want to cut your losses.

What should you do when things turn sour, as they did in October 1987? The answer is to go defensive. Defensive investing doesn't mean pouring all your dollars into a fund with a dazzling recent record. That means buying funds for the long term and ignoring short-term fluctuations. Trying to time mutual-fund transactions is a mug's game, and few amateurs are savvy enough to make the right move at the right moment.

Besides, you don't necessarily have to sacrifice performance for security. What you want are funds that perform well all the time, what we call "all-weather funds." These generally are not the flashy, one-year winners. Look for funds with impressive long-term gains and relatively smooth rides through varying market conditions, funds like Dynamic American Fund, managed by Dynamic Funds Management Incorporated's Seymour Schulich. It had an average annual gain of 15.4% in the past five years, (to March 31, 1988) with less than average variability. Few of Schulich's peers have managed to turn the same trick. However, other funds, such as Viking Commonwealth Fund, which posted an average annual gain of 15.7% for the same five-year period, United Accumulative Retirement (13.9%) and Cundill Security Fund (13.8%) also fit into the all-weather category.

The best way to insulate your investments from volatile markets is to diversify, diversify, diversify. Have we made our point? Mutual funds are by nature diversified, as they hold many different securities. But you can spread the risks even more by developing a mix of different funds to suit your age, income, investment needs, tax situation and stomach for volatility. The quick way to protect yourself is to buy balanced funds that contain both fixed-income securities and equities. The theory is that the bonds, debentures and preferred shares will serve as a hedge against declines in the common stocks. The shares, meanwhile, give you the opportunity for gains when the stock market is booming.

The performance of a balanced fund can be expected to lag behind that of a common stock fund in a rising market, but the balanced fund should drop less when the market is falling.

There's no way of insuring that one fund manager will continue to outperform the pack consistently, so it may be wise to put your money into several people's hands. The easiest way to do this is through funds that use your money to invest in other mutual funds, usually within a single family. One example is Dynamic Funds Management Incorporated.

You can also create your own blend of funds by investing in a family of funds, for example AGF, Dynamic and Investors Group, which allow free switching from fund to fund. But you may not always like the way these families manage their funds. So why not diversify among different family groups?

For the equity portion of your portfolio, consider Canadian and foreign stock funds, which allow you to spread the risks geographically as well as among managers.

To capitalize on a possible interest-rate decline, the portfolio should contain some bond or mortgage funds. Bond prices move inversely with interest rates. For every notch the rates move lower, there's an increase in the market value of the bonds in the fund.

The ultimate defensive fund is the money-market fund, which invests in short-term securities, such as treasury bills and term deposits, and usually tracks short-term rates. Money-market funds can be a good place to park cash, particularly if the stock market goes sour.

Although much riskier, specialized resource funds have a protective role. Commodity-related stocks benefit when inflation heats up. Gold stocks, in particular, are viewed as hedges against rising prices.

But don't buy too many specialty funds. Unless you're willing to put in the time and effort to monitor your investment closely, sector funds shouldn't make up more than ten percent of your holdings.

It isn't easy to pick the right time to buy your mutual fund. A "dollar-cost averaging" approach may be the best way to buy. With this method, you invest equal sums at regular intervals, monthly, quarterly or annually. Your regular installment buys more shares when prices are down and fewer when they are up. Let's say you want to invest $100 a month in Templeton Growth Fund. When units are worth $10 each you can buy ten units a month. If the units rise to $20 you get five units a month. Therefore, there's no worry about committing too much at the top of the market or buying too little at the bottom. The forced discipline of dollar-cost averaging removes a key flaw in the average investor's psyche – the desire to buy when the market is up and sell when it is down. But dollar-cost averaging isn't a sure thing. If you take this approach when shares are riding a crest and prices fall significantly just as you wish to liquidate, a loss is sure to occur.

But don't be upset by the occasional market decline. As long as you keep on putting in your money, and as long as you don't have to withdraw it when prices are low, depressed markets can be a boon to your savings plan.

If you have a high income and know what you're doing, borrowing to buy mutual funds can make you rich. It's all because of the magic known as "leverage," which allows you to make more by putting up less.

Here's how it works. Say you're sure a particular fund is going to rise in value over the next five to ten years, but you only have $5,000 to invest. Go to the bank and borrow $20,000. If you're buying the right fund, many banks will be more than willing to loan you money. Now you've got a total of $25,000 to invest, of which $5,000, or twenty percent, is your own cash. The fund does well, and your $25,000 investment increases in value by $5,000, to $30,000. You've effectively doubled the value of your original $5,000 investment. As well, if you've bought a fund that invests in

Canadian securities, you can deduct the loan interest from your income.

You never get something for nothing in the harsh world of investing. The tradeoff for leveraging is increased risk; leveraging magnifies your losses just as it amplifies gains. In our example, your $5,000 investment would be wiped out if the fund's value fell by twenty percent.

No big deal, you say? Guess again. It doesn't take much to make bankers queasy. If the value of your investment declines significantly, they will probably force you to put up more cash to maintain your twenty-percent margin. If you don't have the cash, you may have to redeem fund units, probably at a loss, to come up with it.

So if you decide to borrow, take note: it's a good strategy when the market is rising, but a disaster when it turns the other way. Moreover, if interest rates rise, higher borrowing costs will cut into any profits you might hope to make.

So, should you lever? The answer is perhaps – but only if you have enough free cash available from other sources, in case your investment declines in value. The most important thing to remember is that you should start counting your winnings and paying down your bank loans if the market starts looking jittery.

If you're willing to go against the grain, here's an idea that could pay off: pick a fund with a mediocre performance record. It's not as zany as it sounds, especially after years of overpowering mutual-fund performance gains. One profitable theory is to buy stocks when they are out of favor and sell when other investors are gobbling them up. The same applies to mutual funds. If you know what you're doing, the best returns may come from funds closer to the bottom of the performance list than the top.

That's not to say you should go out and buy the biggest lemon on the list. The idea is to find a fund with a superior long-term rate of return that has fallen on short-term hard times. Or look for one that has invested in a depressed industry sector, which could turn around with better economic news. If, for instance, you had the foresight to buy into an energy fund in mid-1986, when crude oil was fetching U.S. $11 a barrel, you were sitting pretty a year later when oil prices climbed to $19, and these funds were hot performers.

Stock-picking techniques vary among investment managers. No manager always outperforms the pack; even the best do relatively poorly when their stock-selection techniques aren't suited to a particular market condition. So you should try to buy funds when their managers are at the bottom of their performance cycles. Hold on as the funds climb back up the performance rankings. A strong proponent of this approach is Mal Spooner, a vice-president with Toronto money manager Elliott and Page Limited. He recommends buying any fund that is underperforming the average, as long as you have confidence in the manager.

How do you know the best time to buy? One approach is to learn as much as possible about the manager's investment approach. That should give you a clue about how market conditions will affect the fund's performance. Also, look at the fund's history to determine at what points in the economic cycle it has underperformed its competitors. If you can find a fairly consistent pattern, then you may have something.

This approach probably isn't for everyone. Investing in out-of-favor mutual funds may be logical, but it goes against human nature. Says Spooner: "If you're going to use this approach successfully, you will need a great deal of self-discipline, self-confidence and just plain nerve."

Deciding when to sell is just as difficult as determining when to buy. Toronto financial planner Tony De Thomasis lists five situations in which you should consider selling.

• Your fund is a perennial loser. As we have pointed out, every fund will probably have an off year. But if yours continues to limp along at the bottom of the performance tables for a year or two, don't hesitate to withdraw.

• Your fund gets too hot. If your sizzling equity fund continues to singe other similar funds for several months or more, it could indicate that the manager is taking too many chances with the portfolio. Remember: the higher the climb, the faster the fall.

• Your fund becomes too popular. Top managers who must contend with huge inflows of cash have to invest it wisely and fast, or performance will lag. Many Canadian funds faced that problem during the 1987 RRSP season, when hundreds of millions of dollars flowed in. Unable to find stocks to buy, these funds had to keep millions in low-yielding treasury bills and money-market investments. Performance, as a result, suffered.

• The portfolio manager jumps ship. As we pointed out, an impressive performance record is irrelevant if the manager who quarterbacked the fund quits.

• The economy shifts. If, for instance, interest rates soar, you may want to lighten up on your bond fund holdings.

Similarly, if it looks like crude prices will fall, it is probably time to reduce your exposure to energy funds.

How you sell out can affect your profits. When you decide it's time to leave, don't withdraw all at once: a systematic approach is necessary. Set a clear target for how much to sell, and choose a time period in which to complete the transaction. Then it's easy to determine how much you need to withdraw at regular intervals to meet your goals.

Again, an averaging plan may be appropriate – withdrawing equal sums at regular intervals. Assume you've decided to withdraw $100 a month from your holdings in the Templeton Growth Fund. When units are worth $10 each, you would be redeeming ten units a month. When they rise in value to $20 apiece, you would only get rid of five in a month. Therefore, there's no worry about selling off too many units when prices are high and too few when prices are low. A good rule of thumb is to plan to sell your target amount within six to twelve months, as it's hard to forecast economic trends beyond that period.

One of the quickest ways to make money in funds from 1982 to 1987 was to buy shares in the companies that sell and manage the funds. During that period, soaring stock prices for fund-management companies made the performance gains by the mutual funds themselves look sluggish.

What had made these stocks such hits was simple supply and demand. Precious few of the fund-management companies are public. And investors, it seems, were willing to pay hefty prices for the purest possible play in the fund sales boom.

One thing many investors forgot, though, is that just because these companies make their money managing and selling funds, they are not immune to downturns in the market. When the October 1987 crash came, the fund managers suffered more than most. They dropped fifty percent from previous highs.

The publicly traded companies that sell and manage the funds form a small but diverse group. Mighty MacKenzie Financial Corporation, for instance, has grown from less than $600 million in mutual-fund assets under administration to about $4 billion, largely a result of aggressive marketing and consistently strong portfolio performance. The list also includes the behemoth of the bunch, Investors Group Incorporated, Canada's largest marketer of mutual funds, with $5 billion in assets. Then there is Sceptre Investment Counsel Limited, which has $3 billion in assets, mostly from pension funds.

Even though the fund sales boom has tailed off, the stock price move by these fund companies may not be over. Prudential-Bache Securities Canada Limited investment analyst A.S. Thompson thinks the performance of the stocks will likely become less cyclical in future. Small investors, leery of volatile stock markets, will continue to favor mutual funds because of their professional management. "When the Dow Jones industrial average can go up and down a hundred points in a single day," Thompson says, "I think we will see more people throwing in the towel and jumping into mutual funds." That's good news for management companies, who get paid an annual fee based on the amount of assets under administration. And share prices of the management companies will reflect the popularity of mutual funds.

Chapter

8

The Managers

IT'S A STEAMY FRIDAY AFTERNOON in July 1987, months before the October crash. But the broiling weather hasn't stopped thousands of men and women crowding into the subdued elegance of Toronto's Roy Thomson Hall. Well-tailored and middle-aged, the audience could have been waiting for one of the visiting maestros or divas who normally grace the auditorium stage. But today they are here to pay homage to a superstar of a different sort – John Templeton, president, founder and investment guru of Templeton Growth Fund, and perhaps the most famous fund manager of this or any other generation. The crowd, mostly investors in Templeton Growth Fund, sits in rapt, respectful attention as the dapper, white-haired Templeton makes a short presentation and then patiently answers questions for an hour and a half. Templeton's remarks are sobering: he warns investors to be prepared for a bear market and not to be surprised if their share prices go down. (This was, after all, the summer of 1987).

But afterward, as the audience files across the auditorium's carpeted aisles, his cautious message seems forgotten. "That's why I came," gushes one Rosedale matron, who sounds more like a teenager at a Madonna concert, "I just wanted to see him."

Templeton isn't the only fund manager receiving celebrity treatment these days. Mutual-fund managers used to be dragged out once a year for shareholders' meetings, and the rest of the time they were left alone to manage their portfolios. But now, in the eighties, the boom in mutual-fund sales has thrust fund managers to the financial world's center stage. They are now among the most powerful figures on today's investment scene. With more than $31 billion in assets under administration, they have the power to move markets and the ability to make everyone associated with the funds they run very, very rich.

Many of them start the day with a quick glance at their fund's asset values, listed in the financial pages, to see how they've stacked up against their competitors. There's good reason for this competitive zeal: most managers are paid an annual salary plus an annual bonus based on their performances compared with other funds with similar objectives. These days even fresh-faced MBAs can receive pro-athlete-sized paychecks of $100,000 or more a year, and the real superstar managers, especially those entrepreneurs who started their own funds, can haul home as much as $1.5 million annually, including bonuses.

There's no model for the average mutual-fund manager. Most are male, in their forties, although some are in their late twenties or early thirties. And a few, like Templeton, are in their seventies.

Most managers say their hobbies are solo efforts that

reflect their competitive, lone-wolf personalities at work. Rob McEwen, the boyish president of CSA Management Limited, which manages a family of gold funds, likes to escape on weekends by canoeing, parasailing or teaching downhill skiing. Bob Tattersall, who manages the Saxon group of mutual funds, spent Christmas 1986 on a winter survival course and likes to run a couple of marathons a year. "It is no coincidence," says Tattersall. "To be a portfolio manager you have to be willing to go against the consensus. That usually implies the type of personality [that] likes solitary pursuits."

Carousing with the boys is out. While Bay Street's brokers and floor traders have regular watering holes, like Sammy's Exchange, where they talk shop, portfolio managers tend to be workaholics who only have time for dinner and to read a few brokerage reports and financial periodicals before going to bed.

How good are they at managing other people's money? It's hard to say. Tristram Lett, a principal with Oakville, Ontario money-manager Trafalgar Capital Management Corporation, figures that more than eighty percent of mutual funds underperformed the market from 1982 to 1987. That means you would generally have been better off buying one of the "no-brain" stock index funds that mirror the market average. "In most cases you have to scratch your head and ask yourself whether the big price you pay is worth it," Lett says.

Of course, many funds outpace the averages – but no one beats the pack all the time. Some funds do well when markets are rising but fall apart when prices tumble. Others soldier on during good times and bad. "Asking who is the best manager is the same thing as asking which is the best stock. It is entirely a function of the marketplace," says Don

Ezra, a principal with Toronto-based Pension Finance Associates Limited, which methodically measures the investment performances of hundreds of Canadian fund managers.

The importance of the individual manager varies. The more a fund relies on computers and software-driven investment models, for instance, the less important the individual portfolio manager is. But a portfolio manager usually takes on added clout when he or she is an entrepreneur who started a fund and runs a one-person show.

What separates the stars from the also-rans? They're usually on the job seven days a week, poring over newspapers, balance sheets and brokerage house reports; gulping down coffee with stockbrokers, analysts and corporate managers; running endless spread sheets on their PCs.

But they are also individuals, and their decision-making processes and portfolios reflect their own personalities and philosophies. Some take a "top-down" approach: they determine the major forces controlling the economy and investment markets and then look for stocks that will benefit in response to these forces. Others, including Templeton, favor a "bottom-up" approach, which involves detailed research about particular companies.

Many fund organizations play down the superstar phenomenon. They are worried that if their star quits or is moved to another fund, shareholders will pull out. Others fear a return to the go-go era of the late 1960s, when publicity-hungry fund managers courted the press and lured thousands of new investors to their funds just before the market crashed. Says the biggest star of them all, John Templeton: "The star system is over-rated, plain and simple. Ninety-five percent of my investment ideas come from other people."

But many fund executives like seeing their portfolio managers portrayed as stars. Stardom provides salespeople with good ammunition. Top performance allows agents to sell more shares of the fund, and all those associated with the fund make money. As for the shy celebrities themselves, most realize that they are simply too valuable a marketing tool to be left in the back rooms anymore.

Sir John Templeton is the yardstick by which today's hotshots are measured. From the splendid isolation of his cool, white-pillared mansion on Lyford Cay in the Bahamas, Templeton has built an unparalleled reputation as a fund manager by scanning the world for bargain stocks. If you had put $1,000 in Templeton Growth at its start in 1954, your money would have been worth $1,161,423, after commissions, at the end of January 1988.

That sort of performance has attracted $12 billion to the Templeton International Group. Not bad for a man who was born dirt poor in Winchester, Tennessee seventy-five years ago. During the Depression, Templeton's father told him he couldn't give him any money for a Yale education. So Templeton worked his way through college with the aid of scholarships, then earned a two-year Rhodes scholarship at Oxford. Eventually he went to New York, where he worked as a trainee at Fenner and Beane, one of the predecessors of Merrill Lynch.

The Templeton legend begins in 1939, just after war broke out in Europe. At that time, John Templeton decided to buy $100 worth of every stock trading on U.S. exchanges for less than $1 a share. When the dust had settled, Templeton owned stock in 104 companies – 34 of which were bankrupt. He held each stock for an average of four years before selling. In the end he had $40,000, four times what he originally paid.

Templeton used some of the money from that coup to buy out an elderly investment counselor for $5,000. His new firm, Templeton, Dobbrow and Vance, eventually grew to manage $300 million, including eight mutual funds. Templeton, however, wanted more time to concentrate on his investment practices. So he sold the partnership and kept only the Canadian-based Templeton Growth Fund. Under U.S. laws at the time, Americans who bought shares in Canadian companies had to pay an eleven-percent interest equalization tax. Because of the tax the U.S. buyer didn't want the fund.

Templeton moved to Nassau, built a sumptuous southern-style mansion on the grounds of the Lyford Cay Club – a favorite haunt of rich, expatriate Canadians like E.P. Taylor, a neighbor of Templeton's – and focused his attentions on running that single small fund. Since then, Templeton, a parsimonious, hard-working, devoutly religious man, has made himself and thousands of investors rich by hunting around the globe for stock-market bargains.

Templeton shuns stocks that sell for twenty times as much as they earn, and finds smaller, unrecognized companies that sell for much smaller fractions of their net worth. The best bargains are stocks that are completely ignored by other investors. Templeton calls himself an accommodator. "When greedy investors jump in to buy at the top of the bull market I accommodate them by selling them my shares," he said in an interview in Toronto in 1987. "When nervous investors are selling at the bottom, I accommodate them by buying."

Templeton uses a "bottom-up" approach, searching for individual shares selling at low prices in any country or industry. To know when shares are cheap he uses several yardsticks of value – price-earnings multiples, price and cash-flow ratios, and so on. The guide he uses most often is price relative to probable future earnings.

He bought European stocks after World War Two, convinced that the Marshall Plan would cause business to boom abroad. He rode the Canadian boom in the 1950s, certain that Canada would grow, because of natural-resource development. He emphasized Japanese stocks throughout the late 1970s and early 1980s.

In the spring of 1988, Templeton was again big on Canadian markets. The falling Canadian dollar, in particular, has made Canada a strong competitor and a low-cost producer in many areas. He also liked the look of Canadian banks, which were then selling quite cheaply because of their bad debts. "No doubt banks will survive and in the future they will have very good earnings," Templeton said during a visit to Toronto in 1988. "So we're buying them now when the outlook is full of bad news." Templeton also liked emerging growth stocks, since stocks in smaller companies (or small cap stocks) have been overlooked in the rush for shares of large blue-chip companies (large cap stocks).

It is impossible to separate Templeton the investor from Templeton the religious believer. A devout Presbyterian who likes to open business meetings with a prayer, he now spends at least half his time on church and charity work. And each year on his behalf in a London ceremony, Prince Philip presents the Templeton Foundation Prize for Progress in Religion to the person who has encouraged "the greatest increase in the love of God." Worth more than $180,000, this annual award first went to Mother Teresa of Calcutta in 1973 and has also been won by the Reverend Billy Graham.

Templeton is quick to point out that his firm is hardly a one-man show. He employs nine chartered financial analysts who run quick reviews on an astounding six thousand stocks every year. The team narrows the field to six hundred for "serious study and estimates" before picking the hundred-odd securities that form the Templeton Growth portfolio. Templeton makes the final decisions for the fund, and works closely with the analysts.

His organization is growing fast. One fund management company, Templeton, Galbraith and Hansberger Limited, went public on the London Stock Exchange in 1986. Meanwhile, Templeton wants to spread his North American client base worldwide. In 1987 he added a slew of new funds, among them Templeton Emerging Nations Funds, Templeton Income Fund, Templeton Global Growth Fund and Templeton Taft Philanthropic Trust. He plans to continue to add one or two new funds per year.

As for his own personal plans, Templeton is aware of his advancing age, as are fund shareholders. And he knows that at some point he will have to take a back seat. But that time hasn't arrived yet. "I believe if you have a God-given talent you have an obligation to use it as long as you are able," he says.

Ask **Bob Krembil**, chief pilot of the $500 million Trimark Fund, how he picks stocks to buy and he's damned if he can tell you. He doesn't have strict price-earning ratios or cash-flow multiples that alert him to bargains. Nor are the walls of his office covered with elaborate charts of trading patterns. Press him further and the best he can do is describe his approach as fluid, dynamic and just plain common-sense – in a word, pragmatic. "We think of ourselves as businesspeople more than investment analysts," he says finally, sprawled comfortably in his subdued downtown Toronto office. "When you buy stocks you're buying a piece of the underlying business."

Krembil's *modus operandi* isn't as vague as it sounds. As a businessperson, he looks for companies with competitive strengths and good management. He's also willing to pay for technological advantages. But he doesn't buy every solid company with good growth prospects. He waits until he has an advantage, an original idea or thesis that has been ignored by the rest of the marketplace.

A case in point is Magna International Incorporated, the Toronto-based auto-parts manufacturer. In 1981 Magna was suffering through the recession with the rest of the industry. Krembil, however, reasoned that when the recession ended, the auto industry would be one of the first to recover. When the big North American auto makers started expanding, he thought, they would be forced to farm out more business to the smaller parts manufacturers. Then he looked at companies in the auto business. Magna was a hard-driving, entrepreneurial outfit, and it was being ignored by the market. Krembil bought shares at $3 to $5 each. When he started unloading them in the summer of 1987, they were fetching $35 apiece.

As the senior decision maker on a three-person team, the dapper, soft-spoken Krembil has hit enough winners to place Trimark Fund and Trimark's Canadian Fund among the most consistent performers in Canada.

But Krembil has more than half a decade of track record to call on. The Grenfell, Saskatchewan native got his start as an investment analyst with Excelsior Life Insurance Company in 1964 after a short stint in the corporate-finance department of General Electric. In 1969 he moved to Canada Permanent Trust Company, where he managed its pension investment operation. Three years later he set up his own investment management firm with Russ Morrison, thought to be one of the best and most cerebral portfolio managers on Bay Street. Five years later, they sold out to Bolton Tremblay Funds Incorporated and began to manage Bolton's funds.

By 1981, Krembil felt he was spending too much time making presentations to prospective pension clients and too little time concentrating on investment decisions. So he left Bolton, taking with him two key executives, to set up Trimark Investment Management.

An avid squash and tennis player who likes to get away on weekends to his farmhouse in Beaver Valley, Ontario, Krembil is also a voracious reader whose tastes run toward spy thrillers. Most of his free time, however, is spent thinking about the market. A student of investing, he regularly takes work home with him at night and on weekends. "The portfolios are never totally off my mind," he says.

Krembil's responsibilities are growing. With more than $1 billion in assets under administration, Trimark has about three percent of the Canadian mutual-fund market. And that figure is bound to grow since the launch of new money-market and balanced funds in late 1987.

Despite Trimark's rapid growth, Krembil and his team don't try to cover the universe when it comes to stock picking. Instead, they study businesses they understand. Krembil feels a particular affinity for technology and manufacturing stocks. When he doesn't understand an industry

– gold mining, for instance – he stays away regardless of how attractive the stocks look.

Despite Trimark's success, Krembil isn't letting up. He and his small staff do most of the securities analysis themselves. The brokerage-house reports that come in by the dozens daily are used strictly as raw material.

Krembil stays away from elaborate software packages for screening stocks. Instead, he develops his thesis, makes sure it is original and then looks at the company to be certain the values are in line. Because of the emphasis placed on the business a company is involved in, Krembil makes it a point to build up a rapport with the management of any company he's considering investing in.

Krembil deliberately keeps his portfolios small, with no more than thirty-five stocks in each. He thinks that self-imposed limit gives the fund adequate diversification. Limiting the size of the portfolio also acts as a selling discipline: each time a new stock comes up, the worst performer in the group has to be dropped.

Krembil thinks North American corporate profitability will continue to be strong, because most companies have their costs under control and because the depreciating dollar is causing sales to rise in the late eighties. He is buying stocks in companies that suffered when the dollar appreciated in 1986, and which theoretically stand to benefit from a falling Canadian dollar. Among the best prospects, in his view, are industrial manufacturing companies, particularly in the United States.

Peter Spark is a tall, courtly, easygoing Brit who oozes English reserve; the mere idea of blowing his own horn makes him wrinkle his nose in distaste. "My approach is dull, dull and simple-minded," he says. "My funds have very little risk and lots of down-side protection. But I'm afraid they're not very exciting during a runaway bull market."

He has a point. Spark, like many fund managers who like to buy attractive yet cheaply priced stocks, suffers during full-fledged bull markets, when share prices are racing steadily higher. Bolton Tremblay International and Canada Cumulative Fund, the two funds Spark ran for Toronto fund manager Bolton Tremblay Incorporated, lagged behind the averages during the 1981 to 1987 bull market.

What Spark typically fails to mention is that his conservative strategy tends to pay off nicely in the long run. Spark came by his low-risk approach honestly: he spent thirty-one years running investments for trust companies before he joined Bolton Tremblay in 1985. His reputation as one of Canada's outstanding fund managers was built between 1971 and 1985, when he ran the investments department at Guaranty Trust Company, and his pooled equity funds consistently ranked among the top twenty funds in Canada – and usually among the top ten.

His investment biases haven't changed since he crossed the street to join Bolton Tremblay. Spark continues to tread carefully, trying to avoid what he calls "unpleasant surprises." "In this business," he says, "it's not the big winners you miss but the lemons you end up with that really hurt." Like all value hunters, he looks for stocks with low price-earnings ratios and good balance sheets that offer little risk. In true value-hunter fashion, he sells the popular ones and buys the out-of-favor companies.

Many of the best stock-market values are found among

illiquid stocks that aren't heavy traders. So Spark is patient. He sometimes waits for years before the value of these shares is recognized. Trying to time the market, as a result, is out of the question, since market timers need to hold highly liquid stocks that can be unloaded quickly.

Spark is a strong believer in what he calls "portfolio investing" – that is, owning lots of stocks. The reason is diversification. Spark won't invest more than twenty percent of fund assets in any one industry, or more than five percent in any one stock. He held sixty or seventy stocks in the Canada Cumulative Fund, which he stopped managing in the summer of 1988. The International Fund, which invests globally, usually holds ninety to a hundred stocks.

He likes consumer-products stocks – merchandising, financial services and utilities. But he avoids industries he doesn't understand. Spark likes to keep his portfolios grounded in solid, recognizable names such as Royal Trust Company, John Labatt Limited, Seagram Company and Canadian Packers Incorporated. But Spark's portfolios probably include more than the usual amount of medium-sized companies. Small capitalization stocks, however, are out of the question.

Spark usually depends on brokerage-house reports for opinions on the big, well-known stocks. When it comes to less visible companies, he and the rest of Bolton Tremblay team managers usually do their own research. The ultimate decision to buy or sell, however, lies with Spark, who likens managing money to writing a novel: "There's no formula to it, no mechanical system of doing it successfully."

When he's not busy searching for stock-market values, Spark likes to tend his flower and vegetable gardens. He devours huge tomes on ancient history, along with dozens of financial papers and periodicals. Still trim and fit at fifty-nine, he also enjoys swimming and cycling and thinks nothing of going on a five- or six-mile walk after dinner.

Managing money is a profession Spark arrived at after some disorganized wanderings. Born in Surrey, England, he studied economics and history at St. Andrews University in Scotland before serving in the British Army from 1950 to 1952, mainly in Africa. His tour of duty over, Spark decided the opportunities were greater in Canada than Britain. He left for Montreal, where he joined Sun Life Assurance Company's investment department in 1954.

That turned out to be a fortuitous move. While other companies shied away from equities, Sun Life had built up a commanding stock-market expertise. "In those days, Montreal was the financial center of Canada and Sun Life the best training ground for investment people anywhere in the country," Spark recalls. He spent eleven years honing his skills at Sun Life and six years with a trust company before joining Guaranty Trust.

Spark, who has seen lots of bull and bear markets in thirty-one years, was glad to see the October 1987 crash. For someone like Spark, who is conscious of balance sheets and other fundamentals, volatility is frustrating. In his view, the crash left the Canadian market in good shape: an expanding economy, higher corporate profits and low interest rates. In 1988, Spark saw plenty of stocks to buy. "There's lots of liquidity out there," he says, "and liquidity is what fuels stock markets." On that point, few Canadian fund managers can speak as authoritatively as Spark.

Low-key and methodical, **Bob Farquharson**, the lean, prematurely white-haired senior vice-president of AGF Management

Limited, likes to work alone. He rarely visits companies or assesses their management firsthand. And he doesn't depend upon a team of analysts or on elaborate software packages for help in making investment decisions.

Going solo would terrify many fund managers. It is an approach that costs the small investor lots of money every year. The difference is that Farquharson makes going solo work.

His first taste of running money came when he was a fresh-faced university student working during the summer in the investments department at Manufacturers Life Insurance Company. But life with a big financial institution didn't appeal to Farquharson. So, after he completed a commerce degree at the University of Toronto, he opted for the independence of a small, research-oriented Toronto advisory firm.

Farquharson moved quickly through the ranks, becoming a principal in 1965 and vice-president at AGF Management, an affiliated company, five years later. At AGF, where investment decisions are up to individual managers, he has found his métier. Although his name doesn't always surface when the country's most masterful portfolio investors are mentioned, Farquharson, now forty-six, slim and fit, has blossomed into one of the unheralded stars of Canada's mutual-fund scene.

Under his direction, the $660-million Canadian Security Growth Fund was up an average of 18.6% annually in the ten years ending March 31, 1988. It was one of the best-performing RRSP-eligible funds during that period. Not far behind was Growth Equity Fund, with $250 million in assets, which gained an average of 17.1% annually in the same decade.

What's his secret? Although Farquharson's twenty-five years in the money-management business have taught him that there are lots of ways to win in the market, the important thing is to develop a consistent program and stick with it. The essence of his approach is an enduring belief that, over the long run, investments in well-selected equities will give superior rates of return. He doesn't try to time the market. "In the long term, efforts to evade minor declines in the market often end up being at the expense of benefiting from the rises."

Farquharson takes a "bottom-up" approach to the market: he searches for specific stocks selling at bargain prices rather than looking at a particular industry sector and identifying the best stocks in that group. Of course, that doesn't mean he refuses to change course if the general economic outlook dictates it. When oil and gold prices started edging upward in the fall of 1986, he adjusted his portfolios accordingly, and reaped the benefits. In 1988, Farquharson expected more improvement in commodity prices, which looked good for forest products, oil and gas and precious-metals stocks. "The rest of the 1980s should be most helpful to portfolio managers," he said.

Farquharson reaches his conclusions through meticulous research. By the time he arrives at the office, usually between eight and eight-thirty, he has read the morning newspapers and listened to an all-news radio broadcast. His secretary hands him a brief synopsis of the reams of brokerage-house research that has come in with the morning's mail. The synopsis is a big help when he combs his three stock portfolios each day to see if adjustments need to be made.

He gleans most of his ideas from the dozens of newspapers, magazines and brokerage reports he devours daily, and from talking to the steady stream of stockbrokers, analysts and corporate officials who troop into his subdued Toronto offices. An avid reader and tennis player who spends summer weekends on his family farm near Ottawa, Farquharson usually takes work home in the evenings.

His stock-picking approach is deceptively simple. Several factors are mandatory before Farquharson buys. Stocks must have consistently high rates of return on equity, fifteen to twenty percent, with little exposure to the vagaries of the business cycle. Companies must have a clear advantage in the particular sector of the economy in which they operate, and they should be capable of servicing debt from current cash-generating capabilities. The company's management should take an equity interest in the firm. That indicates they have confidence in the firm's prospects, and is also a clear incentive for the owners to make the company as profitable as possible. Commodity-based companies, such as energy and mining outfits, should have a record of building up reserves, since that's the true test of future earnings power.

Farquharson describes himself as a long-term trader. If things are going his way he may stay with a stock for years. Stocks like Maclean Hunter Limited, Laidlaw Transportation Limited, Dylex Limited, Teck Corporation, Canadian Occidental Petroleum Limited and Pagurian Corporation have been important holdings of his since the early 1970s. If things don't work out – and no one is perfect all the time – he moves on. Whatever path he chooses, one thing is certain: Robert Farquharson will walk it serenely alone.

"Life is a series of routines punctuated by orgies," says **Peter Cundill**, a grin as wide as Lake Superior splitting his tanned face. The line is borrowed from English novelist Aldous

Huxley. But it succinctly sums up how Cundill, the peripatetic manager of the Cundill Security Fund and Cundill Value Fund, looks at life.

At age fifty, Cundill is easily Canada's most unconventional fund manager. Irreverent and youthfully enthusiastic, he works and plays at a pace dizzying enough to make a triathlete wilt from exhaustion. As manager of more than $300 million in mutual-fund assets, he regularly puts in twelve-hour work days. He divides his time between Vancouver, New York and London, logging about a hundred thousand miles in yearly air travel. In between, he still finds time to run ten miles a day and indulge in an eclectic – and occasionally dangerous – collection of interests that includes cycling, skiing, polo, judo and hang gliding.

Cundill's approach to investing is similarly energetic; when he moves, he moves quickly and decisively. Consider the way he shifted funds into resource stocks at the end of 1986, when everyone else was buying industrial companies. The move allowed him to profit when crude oil and gold bullion prices took off. Or consider how he allowed the cash portions of his portfolios to soar to more than 40% by late 1987 because he couldn't find stocks to buy, which left him in good stead when the market slump came. Overall, Cundill Value Fund was up an average of 21.2% annually during the decade ending March 31, 1988, the seventh-best performance by any Canadian-based fund.

Cundill, like his mentor, John Templeton, searches for stocks that are unrecognized, misunderstood or simply out of fashion. And, like Templeton, he has stringent buying criteria. Cundill may be a tad eccentric, but he has all the discipline and patience of a Zen master. After all, this is the man who used a strict jogging regime to slim down from 250 to 170 pounds.

Cundill's disciplined philosophy is embodied in the series of strict rules he uses for finding stock-market value. For instance, the price of a stock must be less than book value (value of assets per share). The shares should be trading at less than half their all-time high and close to the all-time low. He also prefers that the price be less than what he calls "net-net working capital," which he defines as working capital minus long-term debt, intangible assets and preferred shares at liquidation value. Long-term debt must also be at comfortable levels, so there will be room to expand without jeopardizing the balance sheet.

If a stock meets all those criteria, Cundill then looks at rates of past and expected profitability, management performance, government sales, costs and after-tax profits.

Overhanging Cundill's code of corporate performance is a very unemotional view of the market. And for him time isn't a factor. If he buys solid investment prospects, he thinks timing will take care of itself. "That's the Cundill corollary: when it really gets bad and you're really scared, things will invariably get better," Cundill explains.

The strict formula he applies to his investments doesn't always make Canada a particularly attractive market for Peter Cundill. In March 1988, Cundill Value Fund had just thirteen percent of its assets in Canada. It also had forty-five percent of its assets in the United States, seven percent in foreign markets and thirty-five percent in cash.

Spreading his net so widely doesn't worry Cundill, who still runs a tight ship despite the company's expansion. He does all his own analysis, and largely ignores the advice of brokers on the street. Investment ideas come from Cundill's exhaustive list of contacts in North America and Europe, and from wide reading in magazines, newspapers and books.

Of course, Cundill, like everyone else, occasionally stumbles. In 1986, for instance, he bought British Columbia Resources Corporation shares for $2.18. They fetched 90¢ in the spring of 1988. A miscue usually means that Cundill has simply broken his own rules. "When I stray out of my comfort zone I usually get my head handed to me on a platter," he says.

The essence of Cundill's approach lies in financial analysis. And he's well-qualified for the job. Born and educated in Montreal, he received a degree in commerce from McGill in 1960, then spent a year in London and Paris with Wood Gundy Limited, and the Morgan Guaranty Trust Company. After adding a chartered accountant's certificate to his credentials, he joined the Montreal office of Greenshields Incorporated in 1962.

He arrived in Vancouver three years later to take the executive vice-president's post at Yorkshire Trust Company. In 1972, he became president of a Vancouver investment company. Three years later he became president of the All-Canadian Venture Fund, which he turned into the Value Fund. The fund started small, but Cundill made the investment world sit up and take notice in 1979 when he bought three percent of U.S. investment giant Bache Group Incorporated and almost five percent of international advertising agency J. Walter Thompson Company.

Cundill knows he can't do everything alone. He is teaching a successor to take up the investment-management reins when he retires or moves on. The heir apparent is Geoffrey Scott, the twenty-eight-year-old son of Michael Scott, the former vice-chairman of McLeod Young Weir. Scott was working as a broker in Wood Gundy's Montreal office when he decided to pay a visit to Cundill in his London, England office. Despite the age gap, the two quickly found they had much in common, including similar investment philosophies. Some of Cundill's vigor has rubbed off on his young charge, who has taken up jogging and recently dropped ten pounds.

Still, Cundill will be calling the shots for some time to come. And that's good news for investors in his mutual funds, now and in the future.

Chapter 9

The Salespeople

AGE, ABILITY TO TOLERATE RISK and investment goals are all critical factors in building a mutual-fund portfolio. But just as important is finding a salesperson who will help you locate the most appropriate fund or mix of funds. And that can be easier said than done. There are loads of sad stories about investors who bought funds from slick, fast-talking salespeople, only to find that the value of their units dropped like a stone soon after.

One of the important things to remember in looking for a salesperson is that not everyone can sell all funds. Some fund companies, such as Winnipeg-based Investors Group, have their own sales forces. If you've decided to buy one of the Investors Group products, you'll have to arrange the buy through one of their salespeople. Stockbrokers, who sell the biggest chunk of funds, can market a wider variety of funds. So can independent sales agents, who work for companies like Tillcan Financial Corporation or Regal Capital Planners

Limited. Financial planners are becoming big sellers of funds; they also provide a broad range of financial-planning services. In theory, financial planners assess your complete financial picture and determine a course of action that will help you reach your goals. More often than not, their plan of action calls for developing a mutual-fund portfolio.

It would be nice to say that there's a foolproof method of finding the right salesperson. There isn't, of course. But there are some things you can do to increase your chances of finding a sales agent you can deal with. A good strategy is to ask for referrals from friends or financial professionals. Before you sit down to interview any salespeople, do your homework. Read as much as you can about the funds in which you're interested. Become familiar with how different types of funds perform, particularly over the long term. It might also be useful to understand how the commission system works; in other words, find out how salespeople are paid.

But for many investors, what counts most is finding a salesperson who understands your needs and with whom you can build a rapport. What follows is a brief look at several successful salespeople who have mastered the tricky art of satisfying their clients.

Toby Condliffe peers over his half-rim glasses, then grabs his calculator. "This," he says, "is how I sell mutual funds." With his calculator, he can quickly demonstrate to a doubtful client the wisdom of investing in funds. On the other hand, the calculator has come in handy when he has had to explain to an overenthusiastic client the danger of borrowing heavily to make big mutual fund buys.

Condliffe, senior vice-president at Walwyn Stodgell Cochran Murray Limited, is one of a growing army of mutual-fund salespeople who come from the ranks of stockbrokers. And he's successful at his job. In 1987, for instance, he sold $4 to $5 million worth of funds to his clients. Most of his customers are in southern Ontario, but he says he deals with people as far away as Great Britain and Saudi Arabia. He says his motivation is not money. He doesn't deny that the cash is nice – it allows Condliffe and his surgeon wife to live in Toronto's fashionable Moore Park district – but he says his work provides other satisfactions. "I enjoy working with people. I enjoy the expertise I can share with them. It's amazing how little knowledge they have about managing their money."

One key to his success, Condliffe says, is that he works at getting to know his clients. "Fact is, I could open an account and start a trading relationship over the phone, but that's unsatisfactory. I think it's desirable to meet your clients face to face at least once a year." Condliffe attributes some of his success to the fact that he attempts to educate his clients about the market in general, as well as about specific investments.

Condliffe says he often has to work hard to persuade a client, who may be determined to build a portfolio of individual stocks, to buy mutual funds. He points out that he can only keep on top of ten or twelve stocks at any one time; mutual-fund managers, on the other hand, can follow a much larger number. Many investors have to be persuaded that mutual-fund money managers can build a large portfolio better than Condliffe can by buying individual stocks. "I'm out there competing with money managers who spend the whole day thinking about markets. Brokers tend to be on the phone trying to meet their client's needs."

A constant theme in his discussions with investors is the need to diversify. He advises a client with, say, $100,000 to invest $60,000 of his cash in one or two good mutual funds. Then he suggests picking five individual stocks and investing $5,000 in each. The remaining $15,000 goes into cash. "In that way, I feel confident that clients have some diversification, because they have a core position in mutual funds."

The crash of October 1987 has left investors skittish about mutual funds, particularly equity funds. But Toby Condliffe stresses that mutual-fund investing is a long-term proposition. Investors should be prepared to hold on to their investments for five years or so. Short-term market moves shouldn't be a huge concern. Condliffe suggests that holding a balanced portfolio is the best way to weather market fluctuations.

Condliffe argues that his broker's license, which allows him to recommend stocks and other securities in addition to mutual funds, gives him a big advantage over other fund salespeople. Simply put, brokers can offer a more comprehensive menu of investments than most financial planners. They certainly offer more products than those salespeople who can sell only their own products.

While Condliffe *can* sell a wide variety of mutual funds, that doesn't mean he *will*. For instance, he's not particularly wild about speciality funds, which invest in a specific industry or geographical region, because they restrict the manager's ability to diversify investments. While specialty funds have performed well, broadly diversified equity funds will outperform them over the long haul, says Condliffe. He's not sold on domestic bond funds, either; he'd rather buy the actual bonds. The commission charged for buying individual bonds is less than the fees charged on a bond fund. Also, there's a maturity date with an individual bond, protecting you somewhat if interest rates rise and bond prices consequently decline. So on maturity you'll receive back at least the face value of the bond. However, it's possible that a bond fund may fall into a long-term tailspin, and you might be forced to sell your investment for less than your initial outlay.

For Condliffe, a high-profile member of Toronto's brokerage community for several years, selling stocks and mutual funds is not what you'd call a lifelong ambition. His career has taken several abrupt turns, which in large measure reflect three major interests – computers, writing and the stock market. He joined Goldman Sachs and Company in New York in 1966, shortly after he graduated from Yale University. (He was born in New York in 1944.) He worked for about a year at Goldman Sachs before he was drafted during the Vietnam war and spent three years with the Navy in Washington, D.C., as a computer programmer and analyst. After his Navy days, he worked as a legislative assistant to a Democratic member of congress for two years; then he tramped through the South Pacific. His travels over, he became the business manager of a weekly newspaper in Martha's Vineyard, the *Vineyard Gazette*. He intended to pursue his career in newspapers and had a job lined up at the *New York Times* when he decided instead to marry Dr. Nancy McKee, a Canadian surgeon he had met while skiing, and moved to Toronto. His newspaper career bogged down during a stint at Toronto's *Globe and Mail*, and he moved to the brokerage business with Wood Gundy Limited. He was a founding member of Wood Gundy's "42nd Street," the company's most profitable branch. He and three other key members of 42nd Street left Wood Gundy in 1987 to join Walwyn.

Ask **Elaine Andrew**, a vivacious thirty-eight-year-old working for Winnipeg-based Investors Group, about her "customers" and you'll get a hard, questioning look. You can't talk about customers because there really aren't any, she says. "I don't see myself as a salesperson. I see myself as a financial planner. I make sure a financial plan is in progress and that we look after it." Andrew thinks a financial planner deals with "clients," not "customers." But for someone who shies away from the salesperson label, Andrew has done a very good job of persuading her clients to buy mutual funds. In 1987, she sold about $7.5 million worth of Investors Group funds, a drop from the previous year, when she moved more than $9.5 million. In fact, her record during the past several years has earned her a place in the company's Executive and Corporate Division, a financial-planning and sales section open to only the company's top planners. And she's the group's only female member.

Andrew, born in Morden, Manitoba, about ninety miles south of Winnipeg, is also a member of the fledgling Canadian Association of Financial Planners (CAFP), a voluntary group. She's a chartered financial planner, a designation the CAFP confers on those who take a prescribed course or who meet certain experience requirements. "If I can plan properly for somebody, then I don't have to sell," says Andrew, who until seven years ago knew next to nothing about the funds business. She graduated from the University of Manitoba with degrees in education and physical education, and worked for six years as an elementary-school phys-ed specialist.

The foundation of any good financial plan is the establishment of goals, and Andrew says she has to work to help clients determine where they want to go. "Most people don't have goals that they actually follow through on," she says. For most clients, she follows a financial-planning routine that starts with defining goals. Then she and her clients complete a net worth statement, assess investment strategy and determine needs in retirement. An important element is the client's comfort level, or risk tolerance. When the plan is complete, clients naturally ask for specific recommendations about how it should be executed. Andrew, however, is coy. "It's not my money," she says. "It's not my comfort level that you have to deal with."

Still, she presents alternatives to her clients. And, of course, mutual funds are an important option when the client asks about financial products. Naturally, Andrew suggests that one Investors Group Fund, or a mixture, is appropriate. Although she is tied to Investors Group – she can't sell the funds of other companies – Andrew maintains that clients can still obtain reasonable diversification. She argues that the Investors Group family of fourteen funds provides sufficient opportunity to spread the risks. For instance, there's a money-market fund designed for conservative, short-term investors, as well as a long-term growth equity fund for the more adventurous. If you want to select funds from companies other than Investors Group, don't expect a lot of help from Andrew.

Elaine Andrew says that her impressive mutual-fund sales are a result of the financial-planning process rather than a specific sales strategy. "If I can make people feel comfortable with a plan, I don't have to push funds on people."

Andrew found herself in the mutual-fund sales arena more

by chance than by design. After teaching, she decided to travel, and she spent more than two years on the road by herself. Shortly after she returned to Canada, her boyfriend (now her husband) found a job in Ontario, and she moved east with him. She beat the bushes for a teaching job in her field, but failed to find anything suitable. Then she spotted a newspaper ad for a "careers night" sponsored by Investors Group. She went and was hooked.

Her start in the sales game was rather humble. Without Toronto contacts, she began trolling for clients in shopping malls and at seminars. "Your success doesn't come from waiting for the phone to ring," she explains. After seven years in the business, she's now so successful that she generally only takes new customers on a referral basis.

Most clients are concerned about what strategy they should adopt over the next five years or so, given the unpredictability of interest rates, stock markets and the economy in general. But Andrew has no easy solutions. "I try to explain to my clients that there is no right answer. I suggest that over the long run we plan a balanced portfolio that allows them to have a little bit of everything."

What keeps her going? Money is an obvious motive. But, she says, "I don't work for money. I saw a real future in financial planning. I saw a lot of need for people to know what's going on and to at least make educated investment decisions. Maybe I feel a bit like a missionary. It's that education background in me."

Richard Charlton, a young, successful and very persuasive fund salesperson, is just beginning to warm to his subject. Average people, he says, don't understand the economic system. They fail to comprehend that companies are in business to make money. They fail to understand the importance of buying assets rather than consumer goods. And they don't realize what inflation can do to savings over the long term. His patter is smooth, but fast and demanding. He asks as many questions as he answers, subtly persuading you to his view as he speeds along.

It only takes a couple of minutes of conversation with Charlton to realize why he's successful at selling mutual funds. Charlton, the thirty-eight-year-old vice-president of AIC Investment Planning Limited, of Oakville, Ontario, sold about $20 million worth of funds in 1987. His sales during the past several years have made him extremely comfortable. He's got a garage full of fancy, expensive cars, including a Rolls-Royce, a Mercedes Benz and a Lamborghini. "Part of the reason I'm successful is that I'm enthusiastic, and I really care about people," says Charlton, who was born and raised in Kingston, Jamaica, where his father ran an insurance company.

Wealthy, professional clients, particularly doctors and dentists, form a large chunk of Charleton's clients. Generally, he sees people only on referral. His major aim is to insure that clients take a long-term approach to financial planning, and that they "engineer their wealth." That, he says, involves making them understand the economic system and showing them how to make it work for them. "Poor people are frightened of the system," he explains. "They make a reality of poverty through a fear of it."

Charlton says the way to acquire wealth is to do what the big corporations do – acquire assets that produce income, increase in value, or both. "There are only three things to do with money," he says. "Lend it, spend it, or buy something that has the ability to increase in value." Wealthy people, he says, don't have a lot of money, but they have a lot of assets that are worth a lot of money.

Charlton emphasizes financial assets, and mutual funds are the obvious example. But he also helps clients with other assets that will increase in value. Adopting his strategy will help combat the effects of inflation, and in the long run is the best way to insure that retirement is adequately funded, he says.

Charlton, who emigrated to Canada with a young wife in 1973, has several rules for building wealth:

- A part of what you earn is yours to keep. In other words, in any financial plan, pay yourself first. That gives you an incentive to keep on with the plan.
- Buy low and sell high. This is an obvious and oft-repeated piece of advice, but there are few people who can actually do it.
- Establish your goals. Although this is the critical first step in any investment plan, most people fail to take it.
- Leverage human resources. Charlton says you should take advantage of the expertise of others. That's why he's strong on mutual funds, where your investment is handled by an expert money manager.
- Finally, leverage your capital. All corporations use borrowed money to create wealth; Charlton says investors should do the same.

Chapter 10

Looking Ahead

IS THE MUTUAL-FUND BUSINESS going to change as much in the next decade as it did in the past ten years? You bet. Spurring most of the changes will be the heavy competition for your investment dollars by fund companies. But pressure for change will also come from increasingly sophisticated investors who demand better service and products that offer better returns than are currently available.

The fund companies believe there's plenty of room for the industry to evolve. They point to the fact that only twelve percent of Canadian households own mutual funds, compared to twenty-four percent in the United States. And the industry has done a less than spectacular selling job. Consider a survey of consumer attitudes done by Decima Research Limited of Toronto for the Investment Funds Institute of Canada in the fall of 1987. The study of eight hundred households in Vancouver, Winnipeg, Toronto and Montreal with an annual income of $40,000 or more shows that funds are still a mystery to many Canadians. Sixty-eight percent of people surveyed feel the industry has failed to explain what mutual funds are all about; sixty-four percent don't own mutual funds and don't intend to; sixty-three percent cannot name a fund; and twenty-three percent have no idea where to buy mutual funds. So there's clearly lots of room for improvement.

Who will be the new entrants in the fund business? A few big foreign fund organizations like Boston-based Fidelity Management have already set up Canadian arms. Other U.S. and British-based organizations are looking to get involved. The foreign factor could increase even more if the Ontario Securities Commission and regulators in the United States and Britain are able to reach a treaty for cross-border fund sales. That would allow the sale of foreign funds in Canada, and our fund companies could peddle their products in Britain and the U.S.

Still, nobody thinks the big foreign organizations will dominate our market. Canada is simply too small a market for U.S. and British organizations to spend much time and money trying to penetrate. Besides, the domestic competition is already intense enough, says Wayne Walker, vice-president of marketing at Investors Group. Therefore, selling the funds of foreign companies would be a difficult job. "Unless they come in with their own distribution system, they will have limited shelf space," Walker says. Some foreign companies may solve that problem by buying a Canadian-based fund-management company. The existing players are philosophical about the potential of increased foreign competition. "If they help to raise the industry's profile, everybody benefits," says AGF chair Warren Goldring.

The powerful insurance industry, with more than $75 billion in assets, has also demonstrated an interest in grabbing some of the cash flowing into mutual funds, and some of the $300 billion of personal savings Canadians park in savings accounts in banks, trust companies and credit unions. Life-insurance companies have always offered their own "segregated" funds, which are available only to policyholders. But now companies like Sun Life Assurance Company of Canada, Confederation Life Insurance, Mutual Life Assurance Company of Canada and Prudential Insurance Company of America are launching traditional mutual funds that are available to the general public and are sold by the companies' sales forces.

Large Canadian banks stand to be the biggest new force of all. Mutual funds are a logical area of expansion for banks, which are facing heavy competition in the deregulated financial-services industry. By utilizing their extensive branch networks, banks hope to harness the growing demand for mutual funds as retirement savings products. "We see the market potential for funds climbing quite substantially in the next five or ten years," says Bob Boyda, manager of the investor network services at the Canadian Imperial Bank of Commerce. "More and more Canadians are hitting their peak earning years. They'll stop paying off their houses and will be looking for investment possibilities. And they'll be attracted to banks because of their solid reputations."

To cash in on this trend, the CIBC added three new funds to its list during the first half of 1988, bringing to four its mutual-fund family. Boyda anticipates that the CIBC will add a money-market fund and a Canadian equity fund before the end of 1988. The CIBC has already established mutual-fund centers in Montreal, Toronto and Vancouver (with others planned for Calgary and Regina), where investors can obtain advice about fund buying. And, like the other banks, it is working to familiarize staff with the fund business. Meanwhile, the Royal Bank of Canada, the Bank of Nova Scotia and the Bank of Montreal are among the huge banking institutions that have launched funds in recent years.

The banks will exert a great influence over the funds industry by virtue of their growing ownership in the brokerage industry. But, despite the banks' clout, other people in the industry aren't exactly quaking in their boots. Says Terry Stone, head of marketing for Bolton Tremblay Incorporated: "The banks' involvement will just increase the size of the pie for everyone in the industry." But Investors Group's Wayne Walker sees limits to the banks' penetration into the mutual-funds business. Somewhere along the line, he thinks they'll begin to cannibalize their own business. That's because expansion of the mutual-fund business could occur at the expense of other sorts of bank investment products, primarily fixed-income investments such as term deposits and guaranteed investment certificates. Another problem is that banks have only recently developed an extensive range of products. It is uncertain whether they'll want to handle what may be a completely new line of investments.

As for the smaller mutual-fund dealers, all this big new competition is forcing them to arrange hasty marriages to ensure their survival. Local and regional chains are now moving toward nationwide distributorships. Some fund management companies are merging to try to compete. Realistically, however, they may have a tough time doing battle with the big dealers. Says Bob Tattersall, who manages the Saxon group of funds: "Unless you're a niche player with a specialty market carved out, you may be doomed to being an also-ran."

Despite the new investment tools that have hit the market recently, there's room for more. In fact, investors will continue to demand products that provide better yields than traditional guaranteed investments or term deposits. But that doesn't necessarily mean they will pile their money into potentially high-yielding equity funds instead of conservative fixed-income funds. John Crane, director of Royal Trust Company's investment policy group, thinks it will take time for investors to forget the 1987 stock-market crash. "Right now, we're looking at a marketplace that is very risk-averse," says Crane. He thinks this defensive attitude will help determine which type of funds achieve prominence during the next five years.

One thing you're likely to see is the emergence of commodity and currency hedging funds, which will allow investors to protect themselves against fluctuations in currency exchange rates and commodity prices. The trend to foreign investing will continue; global and country-specific funds will grow in popularity as investors search for lucrative international markets.

More ethical funds will be launched. These funds, which use a social screen to make investment decisions, will continue to be a hit. Wayne Walker says that people today "have some concern about the type of world they live in, and they want to be heard."

There could also be a proliferation of products that offer the potential returns of a mutual fund and the security of a guaranteed investment. In 1987, for instance, Royal Trust Company launched a diversified guaranteed investment that puts seventy-five percent of investors' money in a regular guaranteed investment certificate and the remaining twenty-five percent into Royal's mortgage mutual fund. Royal Trust guarantees the GIC portion of the principal. And on maturity (terms range from one to five years), the total return on the mortgage portion will at least equal your original investment. The plus for the investor is that the return is a blend of a fund yield and the GIC yield. The mortgage fund also offers some potential for capital gain, which could be sheltered by the $100,000 lifetime capital-gains exemption.

Venture capital funds, which invest only in start-up companies and have plenty of capital-gains potential, will also come to the forefront for investors who like a little pizzazz in their portfolio. These funds are inherently more risky than traditional equity funds, and are therefore best suited to the experienced investor.

Finally, new types of tax-deferred funds will likely be launched once the final shape of Canada's tax reform is clear.

One thing that is certain to emerge from all this is an increased emphasis on service for clients. Wayne Walker of Investors Group says you should expect to see more professional advice available for investors with lots of cash but little knowledge of the market. "As the marketplace gets more sophisticated, it also gets more confused," he says. Many fund organizations, therefore, will try to transform their salespeople into financial planners – capable of providing a whole range of financial advice – instead of just mutual-fund dealers.

You should also expect to see fund fees come down. But

fund companies will continue to find innovative ways to ding people. Banks and trust companies will likely come to the market with new no-load funds. Generally, though, no-load funds offered by organizations that don't have their own sales forces have found it hard to penetrate the Canadian market.

As the marketplace becomes more complex and competitive, fund companies will fight for sales with slicker, more sophisticated marketing strategies. And that will force the regulators to place tougher rules on the brokers and other sales agents scrambling around for your fund dollars.

As we have shown, there's nothing mysterious or magical about successful mutual-fund investing. All it takes is a clear idea of your investment goals and an understanding of the market and the players in it. Then be patient. You're well on your way.

A Reader's Guide to the *Financial Post*'s Mutual Fund Tables

The *Financial Post*'s monthly mutual-fund performance survey compares funds on March 31, 1988. Here's a quick guide to what each column in the table tells you.

- **RRSP and RRIF eligible.** The R symbol means that an investment in this fund is eligible for registered retirement savings plans and registered retirement income funds.
- **Launch date** shows the month and year the fund was established.
- **Fund manager (years)** provides the name of the fund manager and the number of years that person or company has directed the investment strategy of a given fund. Some funds do not have a designated manager or team. The term "multiple" describes a committee approach to investment decision making. Some funds declined to provide this information.

• **Total net assets** are total assets minus current liabilities; they show the size of the fund on March 31, 1988.

• **Net asset value per share** is total assets minus current liabilities divided by the number of shares outstanding. Investors buy at this value, plus sales charges if any, and sell at this value, minus redemption charges if any.

• **Average annual compound rate of return** measures the average annual change in net asset value per share assuming all dividends and capital gains are reinvested on the date of distribution or realization. No sales or redemption charges are considered in the calculations. Average annual compound returns provide an appropriate measure of comparison with returns on other investments. Investors should examine performance over two or more market cycles of four or more years each. The ten-year average return is calculated from March 31, 1977.

• **Simple rate of return** is the change in asset value, including reinvestment of dividends and capital gains and excluding sales or redemption charges. Examination of annual performance over an extended period is preferable to performance based on a one-year or shorter period.

• **Variability.** This is what the statisticians call the standard deviation and it shows the annual variability of the return. It provides a measure of volatility, and therefore of risk. Funds are ranked as average (avg.), above average (avg. +) or below average (avg. –) relative to the other funds in the group.

• **Reward-risk ratio** is the compound rate of return divided by the variability (or standard deviation). A fund with a high ratio has the potential for high reward relative to risk. Comparisons among mutual funds and between the funds and market bench marks are useful measures of past performance.

A fund's reward-risk ratio should also be compared with its variability. For example, a fund with a high reward-risk ratio and an above-average variability will have had a high rate of return over the ten-year period. But remember, that return will have fluctuated widely month to month.

On the other hand, a fund with a low reward-risk ratio and low variability will have shown a relatively low – but stable – rate of return.

• **Expense ratio** is total operating costs (exclusive of any sales or redemption charges) as a percentage of assets.

• **Maximum sales and redemption charge** is the commission, or "load" paid at the time of purchase or redemption. The word "nil" implies no levy. For life-insurance company funds, this column is omitted; their commission structure isn't comparable to other funds.

Legend

- R Eligible for RRSP and RRIF.
- U US$.
- (a) All invested in All-Canadian Dividend.
- (b) No load; minimum initial purchase $10,000.
- (c) Total assets in US$; NAVPS in C$.
- (d) All invested in Montreal Trust Mortgage.
- (e) Not currently offered.
- (i) Redemption charge 2% if within one year.
- (j) $25 redemption on registered accounts and $10 on partial redemption of nonregistered accounts.
- (k) Redemption charge: ½% if within six months, nil thereafter.
- (l) $10 partial redemption charge.
- (q) No sales charge; sold only to members of the Canadian Medical Association and their families.
- (r) Asset mix includes precious metals.
- (u) Redemption charge 2% if within 90 days.

Compiled by Financial Post Information Service.

Appendix

The Financial Post's Mutual Fund Survey For the Year Ended March 31, 1988

Fund name	RRSP & RRIF eligible	Launch date	Fund manager (Years)	Total net assets $ millions Mar.31, 1988	Net asset value per share	Average annual compound rate of return ‡ 10 yr. %	5 yr. %	3 yr. %	Simple rates of return 1 yr. %	6 mo. %	Variability 5 yr.	Variability 1 yr.	Reward/risk ratio 5 yr.	Reward/risk ratio 1 yr.	Expense ratio %	Maximum sales redempt. charge %
CANADIAN EQUITY FUNDS																
A I C Advantage	R	12/85	Ken Rae (Incep)	12.5	10.20	n.a.	n.a.	n.a.	−11.5	−16.8	n.a.	avg +	n.a.	−0.10	2.80	9.0
All-Cdn Compound	R	10/54	Philip Spicer	14.7 (a)	14.81	+14.0	+9.9	+6.5	−11.0	−12.8	avg	avg −	+0.21	−0.18	n.a.	(e)
All-Cdn Dividend	R	10/54	Philip Spicer	16.4	10.71	+14.1	+9.9	+6.5	−10.9	−12.9	avg	avg −	+0.21	−0.18	2.00	9.0
Allied Canadian	R	12/85	Robin McIsaac (2 yrs)	3.0	4.54	n.a.	n.a.	n.a.	−28.2	−25.1	n.a.	avg	n.a.	−0.26	2.00	nil
AMD Canadian Blue Chip	R	11/85	Midland Doherty (Incep)	9.6	10.20	n.a.	n.a.	n.a.	−11.9	−11.8	n.a.	avg	n.a.	−0.12	2.27	9.0
Associate Investors	R	04/50	G.L. Frazer (Incep)	8.0	6.86	+14.3	+11.9	+10.2	−4.0	−4.5	avg −	avg	+0.27	−0.06	1.78	1.0
Bullock Growth	R	12/70	Multiple	8.7	2.13	+11.1	+4.7	+8.0	−11.3	−13.5	avg	avg	+0.07	−0.11	2.38	9.0
CGF 4000	R	09/71	Bill Moore (2 yrs)	4.3	4.68	+12.3	+10.7	+8.9	−17.4	−18.2	avg	avg	+0.18	−0.18	1.71	9.0
CGF Venture		01/73	David McLeish (2 yrs)	0.4	3.52	+2.0	−4.1	−11.7	−15.8	−22.3	avg +	avg +	−0.04	−0.12	2.00	9.0
CMA Investment	R	03/66	MD Management Ltd.	863.3	28.62	+17.8	+16.3	+16.3	+3.0	−3.6	avg −	avg	+0.39	+0.04	0.75	(q)
Cambridge Growth	R	08/66	Sagit Management Ltd.	1.4	6.66	+16.6	+21.9	+22.6	−0.8	−3.5	avg	avg	+0.44	−0.01	2.00	8.75
Cambridge Resource	R	07/68	Sagit Management Ltd.	0.6	2.71	+9.8	+11.9	+7.7	−9.4	−18.5	avg	avg	+0.21	−0.09	2.00	8.75
Canada Cumulative	R	08/72	Peter Spark (1 yr)	126.2	14.04	+14.2	+7.4	+7.6	−12.5	−12.7	avg	avg	+0.14	−0.15	2.00	9.0
Canada Trust Equity	R	10/59	C.T. Invest. Coun.(Incep)	33.7	51.40	+15.0	+9.9	+9.2	−15.0	−19.5	avg	avg	+0.16	−0.14	1.26	nil
Canada Trust RSP Equity	R	10/57	C.T. Invest Coun.(Incep)	351.0	105.63	+14.6	+9.9	+8.9	−11.8	−17.4	avg	avg	+0.16	−0.11	0.86	nil
Cdn Anaesthetists	R	11/57	Sceptre Invest. Counsel	56.4	9.70	+19.1	+13.4	+12.1	−8.8	−10.0	avg	avg	+0.26	−0.11	0.79	nil
Canadian Gas & Energy	R	03/60	W. R. Farquharson	61.0	8.16	+9.8	+4.9	+5.1	−9.1	−21.7	avg +	avg	+0.06	−0.08	1.76	9.0
Canadian Investment	R	12/32	Multiple	93.4	6.53	+12.5	+8.3	+6.3	−13.1	−15.1	avg	avg	+0.15	−0.15	1.45	9.0
Canadian Natural Resource	R	08/86	First Grenadier Fund Mgmt	3.4	5.02	n.a.	n.a.	n.a.	−15.7	−17.6	n.a.	avg	n.a.	−0.16	0.90	9.0
Canadian Protected	R	12/84	Jean-Pierre Fruchet	7.8	10.52	n.a.	n.a.	+13.0	+8.9	+2.5	n.a.	avg −	n.a.	+0.76	2.00	nil
Cdn Security Growth	R	06/63	W. R. Farquharson	586.6	8.91	+18.6	+14.7	+11.4	−11.2	−12.1	avg	avg	+0.29	−0.14	1.68	9.0
Capital Growth	R	10/37	J.C. Stodgell	3.0	7.95	+14.8	+8.0	+7.1	−6.7	−9.9	avg	avg	+0.14	−0.08	0.91	9.0
CDA Common Stock	R	05/58	Impco Invest. Mgmt(4 yrs)	33.1	13.26	+16.2	+14.7	+13.9	−9.7	−13.2	avg	avg	+0.28	−0.12	n.a.	nil
Chou Associates		10/86	Francis Chou (6 yrs)	2.9	21.84	n.a.	n.a.	n.a.	−2.4	−9.9	n.a.	avg	n.a.	−0.03	1.68	9%
Chou RRSP	R	10/86	Francis Chou (6 yrs)	0.8	10.98	n.a.	n.a.	n.a.	+7.1	−0.3	n.a.	avg −	n.a.	+0.17	0.59	9%
Co-op Trust Growth	R	09/68	Co-op. Invest. Coun.	n.a.	13.01	+12.0	+8.9	+8.2	−15.3	−15.7	avg	avg	+0.15	−0.17	1.35	nil
Confed Dolphin	R	10/72	Confed Invest. Mgmt. Ltd.	6.1	7.80	+17.6	+14.2	+12.6	−6.5	−9.3	avg	avg	+0.29	−0.08	1.50	5.5
Corporate Investors	R	07/31	J.L. Boeckh	12.2	11.80	+13.5	+10.9	+8.5	−5.9	−4.7	avg −	avg −	+0.28	−0.10	1.27	9.0
Corporate Inv Stock	R	04/68	J.L. Boeckh (2 yrs.)	37.1	6.92	+15.4	+10.0	+6.6	−33.3	−29.1	avg	avg	+0.16	−0.33	1.85	9.0
Cundill Security	R	79	Peter Cundill (13 yrs)	18.7	14.11	n.a.	+13.8	+12.9	+0.6	−4.8	avg −	avg −	+0.35	+0.01	1.58	8.75
Cundill Value		12/67	Peter Cundill (13 yrs)	265.3	11.91	+21.2	+14.9	+14.7	+13.5	−3.2	avg −	avg	+0.41	+0.21	1.82	8.75
D K Enterprise	R	07/70	Dixon Krogseth Ltd(18yrs)	5.3	11.71	+16.8	+14.9	+27.1	+27.4	+20.8	avg +	avg +	+0.18	+0.19	2.41	1.0
Domequity Growth	R	12/67	R.B. Love (5 yrs)	10.4	8.86	+1.1	−3.9	−7.5	−24.9	−28.4	avg +	avg +	−0.05	−0.22	2.00	0.5
Dynamic Canada	R	07/57	S. Schulich (12 yrs)	189.5	12.64	+16.3	+11.1	+14.5	−1.8	−7.6	avg	avg	+0.24	−0.02	2.00	9.0
Ethical Growth	R	02/86		20.0	5.70	n.a.	n.a.	n.a.	+6.3	+6.8	n.a.	avg −	n.a.	+0.15	n.a.	nil
Everest Special Equity	R	12/86	John Mulvihill(Incep)	n.a.	10.75	n.a.	n.a.	n.a.	−17.1	−20.9	n.a.	avg	n.a.	−0.17	2.00	5.0
First City Growth	R	12/86	Dixon Krogseth Ltd.	11.7	4.65	n.a.	n.a.	n.a.	−12.5	−16.8	n.a.	avg	n.a.	−0.12	n.a.	8.5
Fonds Desjard Actions	R	01/57		34.3	16.50	+12.5	+6.3	+4.2	−14.4	−14.7	avg	avg	+0.11	−0.17	n.a.	nil
Fonds M.F.Q. - Actions	R	01/87	Placements SNF Inc.	1.5	8.97	n.a.	n.a.	n.a.	−14.0	−14.5	n.a.	avg	n.a.	−0.17	n.a.	3.0
Fonds SNF Quebec Stocks	R	12/86		1.5	8.07	n.a.	n.a.	n.a.	−26.6	−18.8	n.a.	avg	n.a.	−0.30	0.30	6.5

Fund name	RRSP & RRIF eligible	Launch date	Fund manager (Years)	Total net assets $ millions Mar.31, 1988	Net asset value per share Mar.31, 1988	Average annual compound rate of return ‡ 10 yr. %	5 yr. %	3 yr. %	Simple rates of return 1 yr. %	6 mo. %	Variability 5 yr.	1 yr.	Reward/risk ratio 5 yr.	1 yr.	Expense ratio %	Maximum sales redempt. charge %
CANADIAN EQUITY FUNDS																
FutureFund Food	R	04/85	Philip Spicer (Incep)	0.5	6.07	n.a.	n.a.	n.a.	−8.6	−8.5	n.a.	avg −	n.a.	−0.19	1.90	nil
FutureFund Golden	R	04/85	Philip Spicer (Incep)	0.3	7.64	n.a.	n.a.	n.a.	−6.6	−16.3	n.a.	avg	n.a.	−0.09	2.00	nil
FutureFund Life	R	04/85	Philip Spicer (Incep)	0.1	5.42	n.a.	n.a.	n.a.	−17.2	−17.3	n.a.	avg −	n.a.	−0.28	1.90	nil
FutureFund Silver	R	04/85	Philip Spicer (Incep)	0.4	4.56	n.a.	n.a.	n.a.	−12.6	−20.6	n.a.	avg +	n.a.	−0.09	2.00	nil
FutureFund Techno	R	04/85	Philip Spicer (Incep)	0.1	3.97	n.a.	n.a.	n.a.	−27.1	−18.9	n.a.	avg	n.a.	−0.35	1.90	nil
FutureFund Value	R	04/85	Philip Spicer (Incep)	0.3	5.20	n.a.	n.a.	n.a.	−14.2	−16.1	n.a.	avg	n.a.	−0.22	1.80	nil
Genl Tr Cdn Equity	R	11/66	Investment Dept.	44.5	24.13	+13.4	+10.4	+9.0	−12.3	−15.1	n.a.	avg	n.a.	−0.13	1.28	nil
Growth Equity	R	10/64	W. R. Farquharson	154.4	9.60	+17.1	+11.1	+11.1	−21.5	−21.6	avg	avg	+0.19	−0.20	1.63	9.0
Growth Oil & Gas		05/52	Denis Durand (Incep)	n.a.	159.63	+17.0	+8.9	+5.4	−4.3	−9.9	avg +	avg −	+0.12	−0.07	0.08	(e)
Guaranty Tr Inv Equ R	R	01/62	Guaranty Trust Co.	30.1	5.82	+16.0	+11.4	+9.2	−12.4	−15.2	avg	avg	+0.22	−0.13	2.13	nil
Guaranty Tr Mgd Equ R	R	05/65	Guaranty Trust Co.	149.9	4.33	+16.3	+11.8	+8.6	−12.0	−14.1	avg	avg	+0.23	−0.13	2.00	nil
Guardian Canadian	R	12/67	Jim Cole (18 yrs)	40.0	5.19	+15.0	+11.2	+12.9	−12.9	−14.9	avg	avg	+0.18	−0.12	1.61	9.0
Guardian Enterprise	R	11/72	Jim Cole (15 yrs)	51.6	1.04	+18.4	+13.4	+11.1	−5.6	−8.6	avg	avg	+0.22	−0.05	1.05	9.0
Hallmark Canadian	R	07/84	Jacob Greydanus(Incep)	2.1	10.58	n.a.	n.a.	+13.1	−6.2	−7.2	n.a.	avg −	n.a.	−0.13	2.04	9.0
Harvard Growth	R	12/67	Robert Stone (Incep)	0.4	5.52	−1.9	−15.9	−28.2	−57.8	−35.5	avg +	avg +	−0.17	−0.52	n.a.	(e)
Industrial Dividend	R	12/77	Mackenzie Invest. Mgrs.	269.4	10.82	+16.8	+17.5	+16.9	−0.7	−9.3	avg	avg	+0.31	−0.00	n.a.	9.0
Industrial Equity	R	01/69	Mackenzie Invest. Mgrs.	178.2	20.56	+16.5	+15.0	+15.7	+0.4	−8.3	avg	avg	+0.28	−0.00	n.a.	9.0
Industrial Growth	R	10/67	Mackenzie Invest. Mgrs.	1,615.3	14.64	+17.8	+15.6	+16.0	+1.5	−6.7	avg	avg	+0.32	+0.01	n.a.	9.0
Industrial Horizon	R	01/87	Mackenzie Financial Corp.	700.0	5.37	n.a.	n.a.	n.a.	+10.4	+5.8	n.a.	avg −	n.a.	+0.24	n.a.	4.5
Industrial Pension	R	02/71	Mackenzie Invest. Mgrs.	142.9	5.99	+16.0	+15.8	+16.1	−3.0	−10.0	avg	avg	+0.27	−0.03	n.a.	9.0
Investors Cdn Equity	R	09/83	I.G. Invest. Mgmt. Ltd.	150.5	5.77	n.a.	n.a.	+8.5	−15.3	−14.7	n.a.	avg	n.a.	−0.18	1.76	8.5
Investors Growth		09/57	I.G. Invest. Mgmt. Ltd.	421.8	7.52	+15.6	+10.6	+10.4	−13.1	−18.3	avg	avg	+0.18	−0.15	1.33	8.5
Investors Retirement	R	11/71	I.G. Invest. Mgmt. Ltd.	746.5	23.60	+15.5	+12.1	+12.8	−0.9	−6.1	avg	avg	+0.24	−0.01	1.31	8.5
Investors Summa	R	01/87	I.G. Invest. Mgmt. Ltd.	39.7	4.68	n.a.	n.a.	n.a.	−8.0	−7.2	n.a.	avg	n.a.	−0.12	n.a.	8.5
Jones Heward	R	07/69	Gary Canlett	60.0	7.99	+17.5	+12.9	+12.3	−10.2	−11.2	avg	avg	+0.21	−0.10	1.80	9.0
MER Equity	R	02/83	Merritt Easton Rae(4 yrs)	2.1	13.05	n.a.	+11.9	+9.1	−9.2	−14.4	avg	avg	+0.23	−0.09	2.75	8.5
Mackenzie Equity	R	05/73	Mackenzie Invest. Mgrs.	70.0	2.42	+19.5	+15.7	+16.7	−1.7	−8.7	avg	avg	+0.28	−0.01	n.a.	9.0
Maritime Equity		07/66	Scotia Bond Group (3 yrs)	0.5	5.44	+8.2	+8.1	+9.0	−12.3	−10.4	avg +	avg	+0.11	−0.14	n.a.	8.5
Marlborough	R	01/68	Investment Strategies 1yr	3.1	7.52	+12.8	+8.2	+7.5	−8.7	−15.6	avg +	avg +	+0.10	−0.07	3.16	9.0
Metropolitan Cdn	R	02/85	Metropolitan Money Mgmt.	41.2	5.53	n.a.	n.a.	+7.2	−19.0	−19.5	n.a.	avg	n.a.	−0.21	2.00	9.0
Metropolitan Growth	R	12/67	Metropolitan Money Mgmt.	44.9	6.16	+10.3	+6.4	+4.8	−20.5	−19.0	avg	avg	+0.12	−0.24	2.00	9.0
Montreal Trust Equity	R	12/64	Montrusco Associates Inc.	24.5	24.36	+14.2	+10.1	+10.1	−9.7	−10.6	avg	avg	+0.17	−0.12	1.36	nil
Mtl Trust RSP Eq Sec	R	02/58	Montrusco Associates Inc.	87.6	20.79	+14.6	+10.7	+10.9	−9.9	−10.3	avg	avg	+0.17	−0.10	n.a.	nil
Morgan Growth	R	02/84	John Zechner (Incep)	27.5	12.18	n.a.	n.a.	+10.8	−11.5	−11.3	n.a.	avg	n.a.	−0.15	1.95	9.0
Morgan Resource	R	02/86	John Zechner (Incep)	24.0	7.66	n.a.	n.a.	n.a.	+8.8	−6.5	n.a.	avg	n.a.	+0.11	1.95	9.0
Multiple Opportunities	R	08/85	M.O.F. Mgmt Ltd.	15.9	2.67	n.a.	n.a.	n.a.	−6.7	−31.3	n.a.	avg +	n.a.	−0.04	8.60	2.0
Mutual Equity	R	01/85	Mucana Investment (Incep)	68.9	12.86	n.a.	n.a.	+10.9	−10.9	−13.7	n.a.	avg	n.a.	−0.11	1.50	6.0
NW Canadian	R	07/65	Phillips Hager & North	6.0	7.70	+15.7	+14.6	+13.8	−10.2	−13.8	avg	avg	+0.25	−0.10	2.00	(j)
Nat'l Tr. Feb. Pro	R	02/84	Yield Mgmt. Group	17.5	100.61	n.a.	n.a.	+10.7	−2.9	−2.3	n.a.	avg −	n.a.	−0.12	1.50	
Nat'l Tr. Jan. Pro	R	01/84	Yield Mgmt. Group	3.0	105.96	n.a.	n.a.	+11.3	+1.9	+2.6	n.a.	avg −	n.a.	+0.07	1.50	

Fund name	RRSP & RRIF eligible	Launch date	Fund manager (Years)	Total net assets $ millions	Net asset value per share Mar.31, 1988	Average annual compound rate of return ‡ 10 yr. %	5 yr. %	3 yr. %	Simple rates of return 1 yr. %	6 mo. %	Variability 5 yr.	1 yr.	Reward/risk ratio 5 yr.	1 yr.	Expense ratio %	Maximum sales redempt. charge %
CANADIAN EQUITY FUNDS																
Ntl. Trust Equity	R	12/57	National Trust	114.0	19.56	+15.3	+11.4	+9.3	−12.6	−19.8	avg	avg	+0.18	−0.11	n.a.	nil
Natural Resources	R	04/59	Philip Spicer	12.5	5.21	+9.8	+4.7	+5.3	−9.5	−16.9	avg +	avg	+0.06	−0.11	1.98	9.0
North West Trust	R	12/67	Northwest Trust	5.8	19.81	+11.7	+9.0	+8.3	−8.9	−7.1	avg	avg	+0.17	−0.10	2.00	nil
Optimal Canadian	R	12/85	W.F. Procter (1 yr)	9.0	6.49	n.a.	n.a.	n.a.	−11.5	−10.0	n.a.	avg	n.a.	−0.12	1.80	5.0
Pacific Growth	R	04/66	Irv Marus (5 yrs)	10.4	6.02	+10.6	+5.0	+4.8	−18.3	−20.7	avg	avg +	+0.07	−0.15	1.21	4.5
Pension Mutual	R	12/67	Robert Stone (Inc)	0.1	4.44	−3.5	−15.0	−25.2	−53.3	−32.0	avg +	avg +	−0.17	−0.44	n.a.	(e)
Perpetual Growth Fund Ltd.		07/86	M D Management	6.0	1.60	n.a.	n.a.	n.a.	−15.5	−20.0	n.a.	avg	n.a.	−0.15	2.00	nil
Phillips H & N Vintage	R	04/86	Ian Mottershead (Incep)	5.2	11.15	n.a.	n.a.	n.a.	−11.9	−15.8	n.a.	avg	n.a.	−0.11	1.75	6.0
Phillips H & N Cdn	R	05/71	Peter Guernsey (Incep)	23.3	17.63	+16.9	+15.4	+13.6	−6.8	−11.3	avg	avg	+0.27	−0.07	1.18	(b)
Phillips H & N Retiremt	R	12/71	Peter Guernsey (Incep)	14.3	51.54	+14.7	+14.0	+12.1	−9.8	−14.7	avg	avg	+0.23	−0.09	1.26	2.0
Planned Resources	R	02/66	Ken Done (1 yr.)	46.3	10.94	+14.1	+4.4	+1.7	−13.6	−25.0	avg +	avg +	+0.05	−0.11	2.00	9.0
Pret et Revenu Canadien	R	55	Gilles Tremblay (3 yrs)	17.7	9.05	+8.8	+4.7	+3.4	−18.1	−19.3	avg	avg	+0.08	−0.18	n.a.	nil
Provident Stock		12/67	I.G. Invest. Mgmt. Ltd.	68.1	9.48	+14.7	+6.7	+7.6	−15.2	−18.5	avg	avg	+0.10	−0.17	1.50	8.5
Prudential Growth	R	02/71	Prudential Fund Mgt.	72.0	7.15	+15.1	+12.2	+11.1	−15.9	−20.7	avg	avg +	+0.18	−0.14	0.98	8.5
RealGrowth Cdn Equity	R	03/83	Reed Monahan Nicholishen	9.0	14.15	n.a.	+11.7	+13.7	−20.6	−22.2	avg +	avg +	+0.16	−0.17	2.00	9.0
Resources of Canada	R	10/83	Roger Walker	11.9	11.61	n.a.	n.a.	+7.8	−3.6	−10.7	n.a.	avg	n.a.	−0.04	3.19	7.0
Royal Trust Canadian	R	12/67	Corp. Invest. Assoc.	244.3	31.45	+13.6	+8.2	+6.7	−10.5	−14.5	avg	avg	+0.14	−0.10	1.43	nil
Royal Trust Energy	R	11/80	Corp. Invest. Assoc.	55.4	7.67	n.a.	+4.5	+2.6	−3.0	−13.6	avg +	avg	+0.05	−0.02	1.73	nil
Royfund Equity	R	12/66	Martin Siegerman (15 yrs)	852.8	20.18	+18.4	+15.7	+13.6	−10.5	−13.4	avg	avg	+0.30	−0.13	0.51	nil
Saxon Small Cap	R	12/85	Robert Tattersall (Incep)	3.6	9.40	n.a.	n.a.	n.a.	−11.8	−13.3	n.a.	avg	n.a.	−0.15	1.75	nil
Saxon Stock	R	12/85	Patrick Horgan (Incep)	0.6	8.22	n.a.	n.a.	n.a.	−18.5	−17.5	n.a.	avg	n.a.	−0.30	1.75	nil
Sceptre Equity Fund	R	11/86	Sceptre Invest. Couns.	1.1	11.37	n.a.	n.a.	n.a.	+1.2	−8.3	n.a.	avg	n.a.	+0.01	1.93	nil
Scotia Stock & Bond	R	01/87	Hodgson Roberton Laing	24.8	9.58	n.a.	n.a.	n.a.	−6.3	−1.7	n.a.	avg −	n.a.	−0.23	n.a.	2.0
Sentinel Canada Equity	R	05/86	Sentinel Invest Mgmt.	106.4	9.56	n.a.	n.a.	n.a.	−19.1	−19.6	n.a.	avg	n.a.	−0.18	1.84	5.0
St-Laurent Reer. Actions	R	07/86	St. Lawrence Financial	0.6	9.84	n.a.	n.a.	n.a.	−17.4	−13.5	n.a.	avg	n.a.	−0.25	0.86	nil
Talvest Growth	R	07/47	T.A.L. Invest. Counsel	61.7	8.94	+14.9	+13.0	+13.6	−4.0	−7.5	avg	avg	+0.26	−0.05	1.74	9.0
Taurus		10/67	Debra Kent (1 1/2 yrs.)	22.2	4.60	+15.5	+2.5	−1.8	−24.4	−24.7	avg	avg	+0.03	−0.25	1.75	9.0
TD's Greenline Cdn Index	R	06/85	J.L. Boeckh	37.7	5.70	n.a.	n.a.	n.a.	−9.7	−14.3	n.a.	avg	n.a.	−0.10	0.82	2.0
TD's Greenline US Index		07/86	J.L. Boeckh	12.7	5.04	n.a.	n.a.	n.a.	−9.2	−18.3	n.a.	avg	n.a.	−0.09	1.02	2.0
Templeton Canadian	R	05/83	Templeton Mgmt. (4 yrs.)	86.7	5.61	n.a.	n.a.	+10.7	−11.3	−14.2	n.a.	avg	n.a.	−0.12	1.79	9.0
Tradex	R	01/60	Sceptre Inv. Coun.	44.8	7.20	+18.7	+13.8	+11.7	−8.3	−10.1	avg	avg	+0.27	−0.11	1.13	nil
Trans-Canada Equity	R	01/72	Sagit Management	4.6	7.30	+16.5	+23.5	+24.5	−0.2	−1.1	avg	avg	+0.48	−0.00	2.00	8.75
Trans-Cda Shares B		09/44	Sagit Management Ltd.	0.9	76.74	+15.5	+18.1	+21.4	+5.3	+5.8	avg −	avg −	+0.52	+0.10	1.94	(e)
Trans-Cda Shares C	R	12/50	Sagit Management	6.8	12.83	+14.3	+16.6	+18.9	+1.3	+2.4	avg −	avg −	+0.39	+0.02	1.92	(e)
Trimark Canadian	R	09/81	Trimark Invest. Mgmt.	444.1	10.25	n.a.	+14.7	+12.4	−2.2	−10.2	avg	avg	+0.28	−0.02	1.62	9.0
United Accum Retire	R	08/71	Gerald Coleman (9 yrs)	165.3	10.96	+19.0	+13.9	+10.0	−5.0	−4.6	avg −	avg	+0.35	−0.08	1.80	9.0
United Venture Retire	R	08/71	Gerald Coleman (9 yrs)	80.0	11.44	+19.0	+12.9	+10.8	−14.1	−13.0	avg	avg	+0.25	−0.17	1.83	9.0
Universal Savings Eq	R	04/65	Mackenzie Finl. (13 yrs)	118.3	10.95	+18.0	+16.4	+17.8	+3.6	−2.4	avg	avg	+0.32	+0.04	2.00	9.0
Univ Svgs Natl Res	R	01/78	Mackenzie Finl. (9 yrs)	55.9	7.19	+11.3	+6.8	+8.4	+1.2	−11.3	avg	avg	+0.09	+0.01	1.79	9.0
Univest Growth	R	03/70	Philip Spicer	4.1	5.65	+12.3	+9.4	+8.3	−6.8	−9.6	avg	avg −	+0.19	−0.12	1.73	9.0
Viking Canadian	R	09/71	Multiple	205.2	15.20	+15.7	+10.8	+9.5	−6.7	−10.7	avg	avg	+0.22	−0.08	1.56	(f)
Walwyn Cdn Equity	R	12/85	Bill Moore (2 yrs)	1.1	9.62	n.a.	n.a.	n.a.	−19.2	−21.4	n.a.	avg	n.a.	−0.19	2.06	5.0
Walwyn Venture	R	09/86	David McLeish (Incep)	0.9	9.90	n.a.	n.a.	n.a.	−19.6	−20.4	n.a.	avg +	n.a.	−0.17	n.a.	5.0
Western Growth	R	08/61	R.B. Marshall (15 yrs)	0.3	4.34	+2.4	+1.7	+3.6	+1.9	+1.2	avg	avg −	+0.03	+0.10	8.80	6.0
Xanadu	R	04/69	Robert Stone (Incep)	0.4	3.67	−0.6	−13.8	−26.1	−56.5	−33.3	avg +	avg +	−0.15	−0.51	n.a.	(e)
			Average:	92.0		+13.8	+9.9	+9.0	−10.2	−12.9	57.45	84.09	+0.19	−0.10		

Fund name	RRSP & RRIF eligible	Launch date	Fund manager (Years)	Total net assets $ millions	Net asset value per share Mar.31, 1988	Average annual compound rate of return ‡ 10 yr. %	5 yr. %	3 yr. %	Simple rates of return 1 yr. %	6 mo. %	Variability 5 yr.	1 yr.	Reward/risk ratio 5 yr.	1 yr.	Expense ratio %	Maximum sales redempt. charge %
FIXED INCOME FUNDS																
AMD Fixed Income	R	01/85	Aetna Capital Mgmt(Incep)	48.9	9.92	n.a.	n.a.	+11.3	+5.0	+10.6	n.a.	avg	n.a.	+0.17	1.48	4.0
AGF Global Gov't Bond		10/86	C. W. Goldring	45.0	10.29	n.a.	n.a.	n.a.	+10.6	+17.2	n.a.	avg +	n.a.	+0.20	0.93	3.0
All-Cdn Revenue	R	09/68	Philip Spicer	1.8	3.41	+11.9	+9.9	+9.9	+7.6	+5.4	avg	avg −	+0.71	+1.13	1.89	9.0
Allied Income	R	12/85	Robin McIsaac (2 yrs)	3.3	5.85	n.a.	n.a.	n.a.	+6.1	+14.9	n.a.	avg +	n.a.	+0.12	1.50	nil
Altamira	R	05/70	Multiple (Incep)	6.3	6.31	+11.8	+11.0	+10.9	+7.8	+9.9	avg	avg	+0.64	+0.34	1.00	nil
Bullock Income	R	07/79	Elliott & Page (4 mos)	4.7	7.73	n.a.	+7.9	+6.7	+0.9	+10.0	avg	avg	+0.35	+0.02	0.74	9.0
CIBC Mortgage Investment	R	12/74	CIBC Invest. Mgmt.	46.6	11.08	+10.9	+10.7	+10.8	+6.8	+6.9	avg	avg	+0.72	+0.64	1.17	nil
Canada Trust Income	R	10/59	C.T. Invest. Coun.(Incep)	9.4	9.74	+6.7	+8.8	+9.7	+3.7	+10.5	avg	avg	+0.31	+0.11	1.35	nil
Canada Trust Mortgage	R	01/75	C.T. Invest. Coun.(Incep)	126.3	38.48	+11.3	+11.1	+11.1	+8.9	+6.8	avg −	avg	+1.10	+0.65	1.06	nil
Canada Trust RSP Income	R	10/57	C.T. Invest. Coun.(Incep)	170.7	43.50	+11.2	+13.0	+12.6	+5.1	+10.2	avg	avg	+0.60	+0.17	0.71	nil
Cdn. Convertible Deb.	R	02/86	C C & L Investment Mgmt.	17.0	8.58	n.a.	n.a.	n.a.	−3.3	−2.7	n.a.	avg	n.a.	−0.12	0.85	9.0
Canadian Trusteed	R	08/62	C.W. Goldring	351.5	4.67	+11.6	+13.5	+13.5	+2.4	+14.0	avg +	avg +	+0.45	+0.05	0.76	9.0
CDA Fixed Income	R	05/70	Impco Invest. Mgmt(4 yrs)	20.6	60.85	+11.4	+11.6	+12.2	+4.8	+9.9	avg	avg	+0.60	+0.15	n.a.	nil
Co-op Tr Income	R	04/67	Co-op. Tr.Group (Incep)	n.a.	9.50	+10.2	+11.0	+10.6	+4.4	+6.0	avg	avg −	+0.66	+0.42	1.30	nil
Dolphin Mortgage	R	01/76	Confed Invest. Mgmt. Ltd.	3.3	5.13	+11.9	+11.3	+11.2	+8.6	+6.5	avg −	avg −	+1.37	+1.25	1.50	2.5
Dynamic Income	R	08/79	Beutel Goodman (Incep)	89.2	5.32	n.a.	+11.8	+11.0	+6.1	+4.6	avg	avg	+0.63	+0.44	1.00	5.0
Everest Bond	R	12/86	Graham Sanders (Incep)	n.a.	10.19	n.a.	n.a.	n.a.	+9.3	+10.5	n.a.	avg	n.a.	+0.32	1.25	5.0
First Canadian Mortgage	R	07/74	Board of Trustees(13 yrs)	500.5	11.34	+14.5	+11.6	+11.5	+8.2	+7.2	avg −	avg −	+1.24	+0.88	1.08	(u)
First City Income	R	12/86	Laketon Invest. Ltd.	10.0	4.78	n.a.	n.a.	n.a.	−1.3	+13.2	n.a.	avg +	n.a.	−0.02	n.a.	4.0
Fonds des Prof. Bonds	R	03/78	Fonds des Prof. du Quebec	n.a.	105.13	+12.2	+12.0	+12.4	+5.3	+8.4	avg	avg	+0.76	+0.29	0.75	nil
Fonds Desjard Hypo	R	08/65		100.8	4.43	+11.4	+11.1	+11.2	+8.9	+6.8	avg	avg −	+0.70	+1.35	n.a.	nil
Fonds Desjard Oblig	R	12/59		34.7	4.55	+9.0	+10.6	+11.3	+2.2	+11.9	avg +	avg +	+0.33	+0.05	n.a.	nil
Fonds M.F.Q. - Obligations	R	01/87	Placements SNF Inc.	0.4	9.70	n.a.	n.a.	n.a.	+3.8	+5.5	n.a.	avg	n.a.	+0.20	n.a.	3.0
General Trust Mortgage	R	06/72	Investment Dept.	47.4	10.70	+11.4	+12.1	+11.5	+6.8	+6.3	avg −	avg −	+1.16	+0.69	1.22	nil
Genl Tr Bond	R	11/66	Investment Dept.	79.1	9.62	+11.3	+12.9	+13.6	+3.3	+10.3	avg	avg	+0.46	+0.09	1.01	nil
Guaranty Tr Inv Inc R	R	01/62	Guaranty Trust Co.	5.1	4.57	+10.1	+9.6	+9.9	−4.9	+3.6	avg +	avg	+0.32	−0.13	1.44	nil
Guaranty Tr Mgd Inc R	R	05/65	Guaranty Trust Co.	32.3	6.41	+10.1	+10.4	+10.5	−0.2	+8.1	avg	avg	+0.42	−0.00	2.22	nil
Guaranty Trust Mortgage	R	04/74	Guaranty Trust Co.	7.1	10.51	+10.4	+9.1	+8.6	+4.7	+3.9	avg	avg −	+0.56	+0.35	2.27	nil
Hallmark Bond	R	12/84	Jacob Greydanus(Incep)	31.1	10.44	n.a.	n.a.	+12.2	+3.8	+10.4	n.a.	avg	n.a.	+0.11	1.04	4.0
Imperial Mortgage	R	12/84	Joel Remis (Incep)	0.5	9.95	n.a.	n.a.	+9.4	+6.2	+4.4	n.a.	avg	n.a.	+0.44	2.01	8.0
Industrial Income	R	07/74	Mackenzie Invest. Mgrs.	117.0	10.00	+11.5	+15.8	+17.4	+11.2	+6.5	avg	avg	+0.68	+0.61	n.a.	9.0
Investors Bond	R	04/79	I.G. Invest. Mgmt. Ltd.	551.3	4.28	n.a.	+11.6	+12.4	+3.2	+12.1	avg	avg	+0.44	+0.08	1.32	8.5
Investors Mortgage	R	10/73	I.G. Invest. Mgmt. Ltd.	1,123.4	5.00	+11.2	+11.2	+10.8	+7.1	+6.9	avg	avg −	+0.79	+0.71	1.30	8.5
Mackenzie Mortgage	R	12/74	Mackenzie Invest. Mgrs.	127.1	1.16	+13.1	+14.9	+16.2	+10.1	+5.8	avg	avg	+0.71	+0.48	n.a.	9.0
Metropolitan Bond	R	02/79	Metropolitan Money Mgmt.	6.6	2.83	n.a.	+8.1	+7.8	−7.4	−2.1	avg	avg	+0.30	−0.24	2.00	9.0
Montreal Trust Income	R	12/64	Montrusco Associates Inc.	18.4	8.41	+10.3	+12.0	+13.9	+2.6	+7.6	avg	avg	+0.52	+0.09	1.09	nil
Montreal Trust Mortgage	R	12/74	Montreal Trust Co.	18.8	10.09	+11.0	+10.8	+10.4	+7.7	+6.2	avg	avg +	+0.47	+0.15	1.59	nil
Mtl Trust RSP Inc Sec	R	02/58	Montrusco Associates Inc.	79.9	18.09	+10.9	+12.2	+13.4	+3.0	+9.2	avg	avg	+0.59	+0.12	n.a.	nil
Mtl Trust RSP Mtge Sec	R	02/74	Montreal Trust	61.6 (d)	10.11	+11.5	+12.0	+12.7	+15.5	+13.5	avg −	avg	+0.96	+0.63	n.a.	nil
Morgan Income	R	02/84	John Zechner (Incep)	12.7	11.65	n.a.	n.a.	+10.6	+6.4	+5.3	n.a.	avg −	n.a.	+0.49	1.50	9.0

Fund name	RRSP & RRIF eligible	Launch date	Fund manager (Years)	Total net assets $ millions Mar.31, 1988	Net asset value per share	Average annual compound rate of return ‡ 10 yr. %	5 yr. %	3 yr. %	Simple rates of return 1 yr. %	6 mo. %	Variability 5 yr.	Variability 1 yr.	Reward/risk ratio 5 yr.	Reward/risk ratio 1 yr.	Expense ratio %	Maximum sales redempt. charge %
FIXED INCOME FUNDS																
National Trust Income . . .	R	09/57	National Trust	11.8	77.50	+10.5	+11.7	+12.4	+5.7	+8.3	avg	avg	+0.44	+0.23	n.a.	nil
Noram Cv Sec.		01/85	Andrew Willman (Incep)	34.0	12.40	n.a.	n.a.	+13.3	+11.5	+0.9	n.a.	avg	n.a.	+0.31	3.10	9.0
Phillips H & N Bond	R	11/70	A.R. Gage (4 yrs)	44.7	8.78	+11.5	+13.9	+15.9	+9.0	+13.7	avg	avg	+0.50	+0.32	0.68	(b)
Prudential Income	R	01/75	Prudential Fund Mgt.	41.4	5.18	+10.7	+11.6	+11.5	+6.0	+8.9	avg	avg	+0.79	+0.30	1.00	8.5
RealGrowth Active Inc. . . .	R	10/86	Reed Monahan Nicholishen	0.2	9.61	n.a.	n.a.	n.a.	−4.0	+7.0	n.a.	avg +	n.a.	−0.09	1.25	9.0
Renaissance Bond	R	12/84	Renaissance Securities	0.9 (r)	4.86	n.a.	n.a.	+1.6	+4.5	−5.8	n.a.	avg	n.a.	+0.12	2.10	8.75
Royal Trust Bond	R	12/67	Corp. Invest. Assoc.	308.6	9.07	+10.9	+12.0	+12.3	+2.9	+11.4	avg +	avg	+0.41	+0.08	1.12	nil
Royal Trust Mortgage . . .	R	12/68	Corp. Invest. Assoc.	1,029.8	10.57	+11.6	+11.4	+11.3	+8.0	+7.4	avg	avg −	+0.77	+0.77	1.36	nil
Royfund Bond	R	07/73	Ian Grant (2 yrs)	237.6	5.13	+10.6	+10.9	+11.9	+3.9	+7.5	avg	avg	+0.54	+0.19	1.40	nil
Sceptre Bond	R	11/85	Sceptre Invest Couns.	3.9	11.02	n.a.	n.a.	n.a.	+5.7	+10.6	n.a.	avg	n.a.	+0.23	1.73	nil
Scotia Income	R	01/87	Toronto Invest. Mgmt.	17.5	9.87	n.a.	n.a.	n.a.	−1.8	+5.6	n.a.	avg	n.a.	−0.08	n.a.	2.0
Sentinel Canada Bond . . .	R	06/86	J.R. Senecal;T.A.L.Invest	63.1	9.52	n.a.	n.a.	n.a.	+3.8	+12.2	n.a.	avg +	n.a.	+0.09	1.33	4.0
St-Laurent Reer. Oblig. . .	R	05/86	St. Lawrence Financial	2.2	11.55	n.a.	n.a.	n.a.	+4.1	+10.4	n.a.	avg	n.a.	+0.13	0.68	nil
Sterling Mortgage	R	01/76	Phillip Wooten (1 yr)	2.1	5.12	+9.8	+9.1	+9.3	+5.4	+4.0	avg +	avg	+0.19	+0.27	1.47	nil
Talvest Bond	R	04/72	T.A.L. Invest. Counsel	10.8	10.25	+11.9	+13.2	+13.5	+5.3	+11.7	avg	avg	+0.50	+0.14	1.58	9.0
Talvest Income	R	04/74	T.A.L. Invest. Counsel	6.2	10.57	+10.6	+10.6	+10.3	+5.5	+5.9	avg −	avg −	+0.93	+0.42	1.31	4.0
TD's Green Line Mtge . . .	R	12/73	Board of Trustees	63.4	10.53	+11.1	+10.1	+9.8	+9.2	+7.5	avg	avg	+0.64	+0.55	1.15	nil
United Mtge	R	05/76		3.4	5.13	+10.6	+9.6	+8.6	+7.7	+4.3	avg	avg −	+0.64	+0.67	1.52	5.0
United Security	R	09/71	Gerald Coleman(9 yrs)	4.7	4.29	+9.8	+10.9	+11.4	+2.2	+5.4	avg	avg	+0.55	+0.12	1.00	9.0
Universal Savings Inc . . .	R	08/75	Mackenzie Financial	12.7	5.26	+10.5	+13.2	+14.9	+9.5	+10.2	avg +	avg	+0.45	+0.34	1.46	9.0
Viking Income	R	11/72	Multiple	115.7	4.10	+9.7	+11.9	+12.2	+2.1	+11.3	avg	avg	+0.45	+0.05	1.03	(f)
Walwyn Bond	R	12/85	Michael Berry (2 yrs)	20.2	10.15	n.a.	n.a.	n.a.	+0.9	+11.0	n.a.	avg	n.a.	+0.02	1.77	5.0
			Average:	100.8		+11.0	+11.4	+11.4	+5.0	+7.9	20.69	26.10	+0.62	+0.31		

Fund name	RRSP & RRIF eligible	Launch date	Fund manager (Years)	Total net assets $ millions	Net asset value per share Mar.31, 1988	Average annual compound rate of return ‡ 10 yr. %	5 yr. %	3 yr. %	Simple rates of return 1 yr. %	6 mo. %	Variability 5 yr.	Variability 1 yr.	Reward/risk ratio 5 yr.	Reward/risk ratio 1 yr.	Expense ratio %	Maximum sales redempt. charge %
BALANCED FUNDS																
Cambridge Balanced	R	02/60	Sagit Management Ltd.	1.4	6.35	+14.1	+14.9	+17.1	+4.1	+5.9	avg	avg −	+0.61	+0.17	2.00	8.75
Capstone	R	08/80	Hughes, King & Co.(Incep)	9.2	5.84	n.a.	+9.4	+9.4	−12.2	−14.4	avg +	avg	+0.17	−0.20	1.89	nil
CDA Balanced	R	01/78	Impco Invest. Mgmt(4 yrs)	12.8	24.69	+9.4	+12.5	+11.9	−3.0	−2.5	avg	avg	+0.48	−0.08	n.a.	nil
DK All Seasons	R	11/71	Dixon Krogseth Ltd(17yrs)	1.1	3.20	+8.3	−0.1	+3.4	−24.9	−19.8	avg +	avg +	−0.00	−0.28	2.16	1.0
Dynamic Mgd. Portfolio	R	03/86	Beutel Goodman (Incep)	103.4	5.72	n.a.	n.a.	n.a.	−1.2	−6.2	n.a.	avg	n.a.	−0.03	2.00	9.0
Fiscon	R	07/76	H. Christie (Incep)	9.4	10.17	+12.5	+11.8	+11.2	+3.5	+0.5	avg	avg	+0.49	+0.10	1.00	nil
Fonds des Prof. Balanced	R	11/81	Fonds des Prof. du Quebec	n.a.	102.97	n.a.	+11.4	+11.4	+1.7	+3.9	avg −	avg −	+0.73	+0.10	0.75	nil
Fonds Desjardins Equilibre		08/86		30.9	9.69	n.a.	n.a.	n.a.	−4.2	−2.3	n.a.	avg	n.a.	−0.13	n.a.	
Fonds M.F.Q. - Equilibre	R	01/87	Placements SNF Inc.	1.9	8.81	n.a.	n.a.	n.a.	−12.5	−10.2	n.a.	avg	n.a.	−0.23	n.a.	3.0
Fonds SNF Diversified	R	04/68		17.1	9.18	+11.9	+12.0	+11.0	−13.2	−11.6	avg +	avg	+0.22	−0.22	0.10	6.5
General Tr Balanced	R	12/86		11.8	9.39	n.a.	n.a.	n.a.	−0.0	−12.3	n.a.	avg +	n.a.	−0.00	n.a.	nil
Hume Growth & Income		05/85	Multiple (Incep)	54.5	10.15	n.a.	n.a.	n.a.	−26.4	−26.0	n.a.	avg +	n.a.	−0.29	2.00	nil
Hume RRSP Growth & Inc	R	05/85	Multiple (Incep)	88.4	11.18	n.a.	n.a.	n.a.	−18.4	−17.2	n.a.	avg +	n.a.	−0.21	0.90	nil
Investors Mutual		10/48	I.G. Invest. Mgmt. Ltd.	298.7	7.94	+13.7	+9.7	+9.2	−6.0	−8.4	avg	avg	+0.21	−0.09	1.30	8.5
Lotus	R	02/84	M.K. Wong (Incep)	121.1	10.95	n.a.	n.a.	+8.5	−9.8	−10.1	n.a.	avg	n.a.	−0.16	2.00	(k)
Mutual Div. 25	R	01/85	Mucana Investment (Incep)	21.8	11.86	n.a.	n.a.	+10.6	−1.1	+2.8	n.a.	avg −	n.a.	−0.04	1.50	6.0
Mutual Div. 40	R	01/85	Mucana Investment (Incep)	158.4	12.48	n.a.	n.a.	+10.9	−4.3	+0.4	n.a.	avg	n.a.	−0.11	1.50	6.0
Mutual Div. 55	R	01/85	Mucana Investment (Incep)	74.7	12.52	n.a.	n.a.	+10.8	−6.2	−2.5	n.a.	avg	n.a.	−0.13	1.50	6.0
One Decision	R	03/86	M.K. Wong (Incep)	73.0	10.32	n.a.	n.a.	n.a.	−8.0	−8.5	n.a.	avg	n.a.	−0.14	1.90	5.0
Pacific Retire Bal	R	12/71	Michael McManus (1 yr.)	9.1	4.37	+10.1	+6.2	+4.9	−9.5	−8.0	avg	avg	+0.16	−0.17	1.42	4.5
Pret et Revenu Retraite	R	05/72	Gilles Tremblay (3 yrs)	35.5	20.08	+11.1	+9.7	+9.6	−5.0	−3.9	avg	avg	+0.36	−0.14	n.a.	nil
Rabin Budden Capital	R	12/85	Rabin Budden Partners	22.3	6.75	n.a.	n.a.	n.a.	−22.3	−17.2	n.a.	avg +	n.a.	−0.27	1.80	(i)
Rabin Budden Income	R	03/86	Rabin Budden Partners	13.8	5.81	n.a.	n.a.	n.a.	+4.9	+3.4	n.a.	avg	n.a.	+0.10	1.40	(i)
Royal Trust Adv. Bal.	R	12/86	Corp. Invest. Assoc.	134.0	9.78	n.a.	n.a.	n.a.	−1.8	−3.6	n.a.	avg	n.a.	−0.04	n.a.	nil
Royal Trust Adv. Grth		12/86	Corp. Invest. Assoc.	18.5	9.79	n.a.	n.a.	n.a.	−5.2	−9.0	n.a.	avg	n.a.	−0.09	n.a.	nil
Royal Trust Adv. Inc.	R	12/86	Corp. Invest. Assoc.	67.6	9.50	n.a.	n.a.	n.a.	−0.2	+1.2	n.a.	avg −	n.a.	−0.00	n.a.	nil
Saxon Balanced	R	12/85	Patrick Horgan (Incep)	1.0	8.54	n.a.	n.a.	n.a.	−19.2	−16.5	n.a.	avg	n.a.	−0.31	1.75	nil
Sceptre Balanced	R	11/85	Sceptre Invest. Couns.	19.3	11.61	n.a.	n.a.	n.a.	−0.4	−1.2	n.a.	avg	n.a.	−0.00	1.80	nil
St-Laurent Reer. Diversifee	R	05/86	St. Lawrence Financial	2.7	11.28	n.a.	n.a.	n.a.	+1.1	+6.7	n.a.	avg −	n.a.	+0.04	0.02	nil
Sunset Fund	R	10/85	C C & L Investment Mgmt.	147.0	11.86	n.a.	n.a.	n.a.	−0.9	+0.1	n.a.	avg	n.a.	−0.02	2.00	9.0
Talvest Diversified	R	03/86	T.A.L. Invest. Counsel	18.4	5.68	n.a.	n.a.	n.a.	+2.0	+3.1	n.a.	avg	n.a.	+0.05	1.73	9.0
Waltaine Balanced	R	46	Hodgson Roberton Laing	31.5	10.08	+15.0	+11.2	+10.8	−1.1	+0.6	avg	avg −	+0.38	−0.04	1.75	nil
			Average:	51.9		+11.8	+9.9	+10.0	−6.4	−5.7	36.37	47.59	+0.38	−0.10		

Fund name	RRSP & RRIF eligible	Launch date	Fund manager (Years)	Total net assets $ millions	Net asset value per share	Average annual compound rate of return ‡ 10 yr.	5 yr.	3 yr.	Simple rates of return 1 yr.	6 mo.	Variability 5 yr.	1 yr.	Reward/risk ratio 5 yr.	1 yr.	Expense ratio %	Maximum sales redempt. charge %
				Mar.31, 1988		%			%							
DIVIDEND FUNDS																
AGF Pfd.	R	07/84	C.W. Goldring	285.3	9.86	n.a.	n.a.	+11.2	+9.7	+11.4	n.a.	avg	n.a.	+0.37	0.77	4.0
AMD Dividend	R	01/85	Midland Doherty (Incep)	13.5	9.47	n.a.	n.a.	+6.8	+1.8	+3.4	n.a.	avg −	n.a.	+0.10	1.69	4.0
Allied Dividend	R	10/85	Robin McIsaac (2 yrs)	2.1	4.68	n.a.	n.a.	n.a.	−0.5	+3.4	n.a.	avg	n.a.	−0.02	1.50	nil
B Tremblay Pref Income	R	11/76	Jean LucLandry (2 yrs)	77.3	10.39	+9.5	+7.5	+7.5	+1.9	+2.7	avg −	avg	+0.40	+0.08	1.06	5.0
Bullock Dividend	R	04/85	Multiple	8.6	9.71	n.a.	n.a.	n.a.	−3.4	+0.6	n.a.	avg	n.a.	−0.09	1.65	9.0
Cdn. Convertible Pfd	R	12/85	C C & L Investment Mgmt.	11.0	8.90	n.a.	n.a.	n.a.	+1.6	−3.4	n.a.	avg +	n.a.	+0.03	0.85	9.0
Dynamic Dividend		09/85	Beutel Goodman (Incep)	11.7	5.10	n.a.	n.a.	n.a.	+12.8	+12.4	n.a.	avg	n.a.	+0.37	1.25	5.0
Guardian Pref. Dividend	R	10/85	J. Cole (1 yr.)	18.7	9.28	n.a.	n.a.	n.a.	+3.2	+3.3	n.a.	avg −	n.a.	+0.17	n.a.	4.0
Investors Dividend		11/61	I.G. Invest. Mgmt. Ltd.	1,041.0	8.80	+11.9	+9.9	+9.4	+0.2	+2.5	avg	avg	+0.38	−0.00	1.27	8.5
Montreal Tr Dividend	R	10/86	Montrusco Assoc. Inc.	11.7	9.24	n.a.	n.a.	n.a.	−1.9	+0.7	n.a.	avg	n.a.	−0.06	n.a.	nil
Morgan Dividend	R	02/86	John Zechner (Incep)	5.7	5.40	n.a.	n.a.	n.a.	−3.3	−5.2	n.a.	avg +	n.a.	−0.07	1.95	9.0
Mutual Dividend	R	01/86	Mucana Investment (Incep)	10.8	9.97	n.a.	n.a.	n.a.	+3.2	+4.1	n.a.	avg −	n.a.	+0.21	n.a.	6.0
Phillips H & N Div		06/77	William Slater (Incep)	10.7	13.93	+12.6	+11.5	+12.3	+2.2	+0.1	avg +	avg +	+0.32	+0.03	0.80	(b)
Prudential Dividend		11/86	Prudential Fund Mgt.(1yr)	4.1	5.09	n.a.	n.a.	n.a.	+7.2	+4.6	n.a.	avg	n.a.	+0.22	1.00	8.5
Royal Trust Preferred		10/85	Corp. Invest. Assoc.	17.2	9.50	n.a.	n.a.	n.a.	+0.2	+4.2	n.a.	avg	n.a.	−0.00	1.77	nil
Viking Dividend	R	06/78	Multiple (4 yrs)	133.5	7.32	n.a.	+12.0	+10.7	−0.3	+1.3	avg	avg	+0.44	−0.00	1.00	(f)
Waltaine Convertible Pref.	R	12/85	Hodgson Roberton Laing	13.3	8.85	n.a.	n.a.	n.a.	−4.5	−3.9	n.a.	avg +	n.a.	−0.09	1.00	nil
Waltaine Income	R	10/85	Hodgson Roberton Laing	25.6	9.10	n.a.	n.a.	n.a.	+2.7	+3.9	n.a.	avg −	n.a.	+0.16	0.75	nil
Walwyn Preferred	R	12/85	Laird Grantham (2 yrs)	10.8	10.18	n.a.	n.a.	n.a.	+1.5	+2.4	n.a	avg	n.a.	+0.04	2.02	5.0
			Average:	90.1		+11.3	+10.2	+9.7	+1.8	+2.6	26.80	31.37	+0.39	+0.09		

Fund name	RRSP & RRIF eligible	Launch date	Fund manager (Years)	Total net assets $ millions Mar.31, 1988	Net asset value per share Mar.31, 1988	Average annual compound rate of return ‡ 10 yr. %	Average annual compound rate of return 5 yr. %	Average annual compound rate of return 3 yr. %	Simple rates of return 1 yr. %	Simple rates of return 6 mo. %	Variability 5 yr.	Variability 1 yr.	Reward/risk ratio 5 yr.	Reward/risk ratio 1 yr.	Expense ratio %	Maximum sales redempt. charge %
MONEY MARKET FUNDS																
AGF Money Market	R	12/75	C.W. Goldring	98.5	10.00	+11.3	+9.2	+8.7	+8.2	+4.2	avg	avg	+8.36	+13.01	0.61	nil
AMD Money Market	R	01/85	Aetna Capital Mgmt(Incep)	64.5	10.00	n.a.	n.a.	+9.1	+8.1	+4.1	n.a.	avg	n.a.	+16.87	0.77	1.0
Allied Money	R	10/85	Robin McIsaac (2 yrs)	22.7	5.00	n.a.	n.a.	n.a.	+7.0	+3.2	n.a.	avg	n.a.	+3.22	1.00	nil
AMD US Dollar Money Mkt	R U	04/87	Federated Investrs(Incep)	10.8	1.00	n.a.	n.a.	n.a.	n.a.	+3.0	n.a.	n.a.	n.a.	n.a.	0.69	1.0
B Tremblay Money	R	02/82	Guy Senacal (4 yrs)	150.9	1.00	n.a.	+9.2	+8.8	+8.4	+4.4	avg	avg	+8.28	+13.33	0.50	2.0
CMA S-T Deposit	R	02/75	MD Management Ltd.	115.7	35.70	+10.9	+8.8	+8.1	+7.6	+3.9	avg	avg	+6.71	+8.63	0.75	(q)
CDA Money Market	R	11/72	Impco Invest. Mgmt(4 yrs)	14.9	39.99	+10.7	+9.2	+8.6	+7.6	+4.2	avg +	avg	+4.22	+2.78	n.a.	nil
Central Money Market . . .		09/86	Central Cap. Mgmt.	38.9	100.00	n.a.	n.a.	n.a.	+8.6	+5.1	n.a.	avg	n.a.	+2.79	n.a.	nil
Dynamic Money Market . .	R	04/84	Beutel Goodman (Incep)	22.7	10.00	n.a.	n.a.	+8.2	+8.0	+4.2	n.a.	avg	n.a.	+9.52	0.75	2.0
Elliott & Page Money	R	07/84	David Roy DeGrasse	49.4	1.00	n.a.	n.a.	+9.8	+9.1	+4.8	n.a.	avg	n.a.	+3.88	0.08	nil
Everest Short Term Asset	R	12/86	Graham Sanders (Incep)	n.a.	10.02	n.a.	n.a.	n.a.	+6.5	+2.7	n.a.	avg +	n.a.	+0.27	0.60	nil
General Tr Money Mkt . . .	R	12/86		12.3	10.33	n.a.	n.a.	n.a.	+12.0	+7.8	n.a.	avg +	n.a.	+1.46	n.a.	nil
Guardian S-T Money	R	12/67	L. Kennedy	33.5	10.00	+10.7	+9.2	+8.7	+8.2	+4.4	avg	avg	+6.38	+4.27	0.50	nil
Industrial Cash Mgmt. . . .	R	09/84	Mackenzie Financial Corp.	72.8	10.00	n.a.	n.a.	+8.5	+7.8	+4.0	n.a.	avg	n.a.	+13.22	0.50	2%
Investors Money Mkt	R	05/85	I.G. Invest. Mgmt. Ltd.	137.4	1.00	n.a.	n.a.	n.a.	+7.9	+4.2	n.a.	avg	n.a.	+10.12	1.07	nil
MER Money Market	R	02/83	Merritt Easton Rae(4 yrs)	0.2	10.00	n.a.	+8.1	+7.1	+4.4	+1.5	avg +	avg	+3.53	+2.26	1.02	nil
Mutual Money Market . . .	R	01/85	Mucana Investment (Incep)	45.8	1.00	n.a.	n.a.	+7.7	+6.8	+3.8	n.a.	avg	n.a.	+3.38	1.50	nil
Prudential Money Market .	R	11/86	Prudential Fund Mgt(1 yr)	63.3	10.00	n.a.	n.a.	n.a.	+8.5	+4.4	n.a.	avg	n.a.	+10.89	0.66	nil
Royfund Money Market . .	R	12/86	United Bond & Share	106.4	10.00	n.a.	n.a.	n.a.	+7.5	+3.8	n.a.	avg	n.a.	+13.88	n.a.	nil
Sentinel Money Market . .	R	01/87	Yield Management Grp.	108.7	10.00	n.a.	n.a.	n.a.	+5.3	+1.4	n.a.	avg	n.a.	+1.40	0.67	nil
St-Laur.Reer Epargne Plus	R	07/86	St. Lawrence Financial	0.4	11.62	n.a.	n.a.	n.a.	+8.3	+4.8	n.a.	avg	n.a.	+2.44	0.49	nil
Talvest Money	R	03/86	T.A.L. Invest. Counsel	2.4	10.00	n.a.	n.a.	n.a.	+2.1	+2.1	n.a.	avg	n.a.	+0.56	0.87	2.0
Trimark Interest	R	12/86	Trimark Invest. Mgmt.	23.5	10.00	n.a.	n.a.	n.a.	+8.3	+4.3	n.a.	avg	n.a.	+13.83	0.75	2.0
Walwyn Money Market . .	R	12/85	Michael Berry (2 yrs)	12.8	10.00	n.a.	n.a.	n.a.	+7.4	+3.9	n.a.	avg	n.a.	+9.86	1.49	5.0
			Average:	52.5		+10.9	+9.0	+8.5	+7.5	+3.9	1.57	2.87	+6.25	+7.04		
REAL ESTATE FUNDS																
Counsel Tr Real Estate . . .	R	12/84		75.9	16.63	n.a.	n.a.	+16.5	+15.1	+9.8	n.a.	avg	n.a.	+1.45	n.a.	
First City Realfund	R	03/83	First City Devel.(Incep)	33.7	5.93	n.a.	+11.7	+14.0	+16.2	+6.5	avg	avg	+0.54	+0.72	1.79	8.0
Imperial Realty Growth . . .	R	03/84	Joel Remis (Incep)	9.9	11.09	n.a.	n.a.	+15.5	+17.7	+6.8	n.a.	avg ÷	n.a.	+0.58	2.22	8.0
Investors Real Property . .	R	11/83	I.G. Invest. Mgmt. Ltd.	170.0	5.28	n.a.	n.a.	+9.5	+8.4	+3.1	n.a.	avg −	n.a.	+1.33	1.58	8.5
MD Realty A	R	06/83	M D Management Ltd.	81.0	128.12	n.a.	n.a.	+10.3	+13.8	+2.6	n.a.	avg	n.a.	+0.51	n.a.	(q)
			Average:	74.1		n.a.	+11.7	+13.2	+14.2	+5.8	21.51	19.29	+0.54	+0.92		

Fund name	RRSP & RRIF eligible	Launch date	Fund manager (Years)	Total net assets $ millions	Net asset value per share Mar.31, 1988	Average annual compound rate of return ‡ 10 yr. %	5 yr. %	3 yr. %	Simple rates of return 1 yr. %	6 mo. %	Variability 5 yr.	1 yr.	Reward/risk ratio 5 yr.	1 yr.	Expense ratio %	Maximum sales redempt. charge %
PRECIOUS METAL FUNDS																
Dynamic Precious Metal	R	04/86	Beutel Goodman (Incep)	32.7	1.23	n.a.	n.a.	n.a.	−3.1	−16.7	n.a.	avg	n.a.	−0.03	2.00	9.0
Goldfund		03/67	CSA Mgmt. Ltd.	13.7	5.98	+18.3	+6.3	+13.4	−16.0	−25.8	avg +	avg +	+0.06	−0.13	2.25	9.0
Goldtrust	R	05/75	CSA Mgmt. Ltd.	38.1	6.25	+13.3	+7.8	+14.9	−15.0	−22.4	avg	avg	+0.09	−0.16	1.86	9.0
			Average:	28.2		+15.8	+7.1	+14.2	−11.4	−21.6	86.97	103.47	+0.08	−0.11		
JAPANESE EQUITY FUNDS																
AGF Japan		01/69	R.J. Whiting	105.3	6.55	+23.5	+35.2	+42.5	+28.9	+2.3	avg +	avg +	+0.52	+0.30	1.56	9.0
Investors Japanese		03/71	I.G. Invest. Mgmt. Ltd.	194.6	16.47	+21.6	+32.2	+41.1	+32.3	+10.4	avg	avg −	+0.49	+0.50	1.32	8.5
Royal Trust Japanese		05/85	Corp. Invest. Assoc.	21.4	21.68	n.a.	n.a.	n.a.	+23.3	+10.3	n.a.	avg	n.a.	+0.31	3.08	nil
			Average:	107.1		+22.6	+33.7	+41.8	+28.2	+7.7	66.08	77.78	+0.51	+0.37		
U.S. EQUITY FUNDS																
AGF Special		09/68	R.J. Whiting	187.2	4.63	+21.8	+10.8	+10.4	−8.3	−15.9	avg	avg	+0.17	−0.09	1.48	9.0
AMD American Blue Chip		11/85	Federated Research(Incep)	4.8	9.01	n.a.	n.a.	n.a.	−16.3	−21.0	n.a.	avg	n.a.	−0.19	2.58	9.0
American Growth		04/57	W.D. Cameron	107.5	7.30	+18.1	+11.0	+8.2	−7.9	−16.0	avg	avg	+0.17	−0.08	1.48	9.0
Bullock American		10/77	Equit. Inv. Mgmt (2 yrs)	32.5	7.24	+12.5	+11.4	+15.6	−16.4	−28.8	avg +	avg +	+0.13	−0.12	1.34	9.0
Canada Tr N American		12/67	C.T. Invest. Coun.(Incep)	17.6	25.91	+15.3	+9.4	+7.1	−14.5	−20.4	avg	avg	+0.16	−0.16	1.38	nil
Century D.J. Fund		04/86	MagnaTrends Asset Mgmt	2.1	8.71	n.a.	n.a.	n.a.	−19.1	−23.8	n.a.	avg	n.a.	−0.22	1.80	9.0
DK American		12/74	Dixon Krogseth (14 yrs.)	0.6	18.68	+10.8	+4.2	+5.5	−23.8	−26.3	avg	avg	+0.05	−0.26	2.88	1.0
Dynamic American		08/79	S. Schulich	75.3	7.37	n.a.	+15.4	+12.6	−2.4	−14.7	avg −	avg	+0.28	−0.02	2.00	9.0
Formula Growth		06/60	J.W. Dobson (Incep)	n.a.	536.90	+22.1	+7.8	+8.3	−20.1	−24.1	avg +	avg +	+0.08	−0.15	1.48	(e)
Genl Tr U.S. Equity		06/83	Investment Dept.	15.1	13.40	n.a.	n.a.	+10.9	−20.1	−26.3	n.a.	avg	n.a.	−0.22	1.27	nil
Guardian Growth		12/67	P. Dietche (1 yr.)	24.2	17.33	+13.1	+4.8	+5.5	−11.4	−21.0	avg	avg	+0.08	−0.12	1.00	9.0
Guardian N American		12/67	J. Priestman	2.5	4.39	+12.0	+1.5	−1.2	−31.9	−25.3	avg	avg	+0.02	−0.29	1.00	9.0
Industrial American		07/75	Mackenzie Invest. Mgrs.	424.6	7.30	+19.0	+13.2	+12.0	−6.6	−16.4	avg	avg	+0.21	−0.06	n.a.	9.0
Investors Int'l		11/61	I.G. Invest. Mgmt. Ltd.	193.0	9.57	+14.5	+10.2	+9.4	−10.6	−21.8	avg	avg	+0.15	−0.10	1.35	8.5
Jones Heward American		02/83	Gary Canlett	4.4	6.68	n.a.	+11.2	+9.1	−13.7	−21.9	avg	avg	+0.16	−0.13	2.50	9.0
Metropolitan Collective Mut		12/67	Metropolitan Money Mgmt	36.9	14.14	+14.1	+4.7	−0.7	−28.6	−29.1	avg	avg	+0.07	−0.31	2.00	9.0
Metropolitan Speculators		10/85	Metropolitan Money Mgmt.	4.5	6.42	n.a.	n.a.	n.a.	−16.4	−20.5	n.a.	avg	n.a.	−0.19	2.00	9.0
Metropolitan Venture		04/70	Metropolitan Money Mgmt.	40.8	8.36	+12.8	+6.0	+7.7	−20.1	−27.4	avg	avg	+0.09	−0.21	2.00	9.0
Mutual Amerifund		01/86	Mucana Investment (Incep)	8.4	10.72	n.a.	n.a.	n.a.	−4.8	−14.6	n.a.	avg	n.a.	−0.04	n.a.	6.0
NW Equity		01/70	Phillips Hager & North	1.9	9.39	+13.6	+6.9	+3.9	−14.3	−22.5	avg	avg	+0.10	−0.13	2.00	(l)
Natrusco		02/64	National Trust (3 yrs.)	13.3	7.07	+12.9	+10.4	+8.4	−13.8	−23.2	avg	avg	+0.16	−0.12	1.50	nil
Pacific US Growth		09/67	Mark Thomson (6 mos.)	7.0	3.74	+6.3	+0.8	+2.2	−20.1	−25.0	avg	avg	+0.01	−0.18	1.29	4.5
Phillips H & N U.S.		08/64	Rudy North (Incep)	28.7	21.97	+16.9	+8.7	+7.7	−9.5	−21.2	avg	avg	+0.12	−0.08	1.18	(b)
Pret et Revenu Americain		08/68	Gilles Tremblay (3 yrs)	4.2	23.43	+10.7	+7.6	+7.7	−23.2	−27.5	avg	avg	+0.12	−0.25	n.a.	nil
RealGrowth Amer. Trend		10/86	Reed Monahan Nicholishen	0.7	5.09	n.a.	n.a.	n.a.	−10.8	−43.6	n.a.	avg +	n.a.	−0.05	2.00	9.0
Royal Trust American		12/67	Corp. Invest. Assoc.	50.5	19.66	+12.1	+9.3	+9.6	−11.6	−21.7	avg	avg	+0.15	−0.13	1.48	nil
Salamander Trust	U	05/84	J.P. Fruchet	0.8	98.35	n.a.	n.a.	+11.0	+0.9	+0.6	n.a.	avg −	n.a.	+0.07	1.25	nil
Talvest American		03/86	T.A.L. Invest. Counsel	5.3	4.87	n.a.	n.a.	n.a.	−14.8	−21.2	n.a.	avg	n.a.	−0.17	1.75	9.0
United American		06/67	Gerald Coleman (9 yrs)	24.0	5.45	+14.1	+11.3	+5.9	−16.2	−20.0	avg −	avg	+0.21	−0.18	1.89	9.0
United Venture		11/66	Gerald Coleman (9 yrs)	27.2	7.54	+15.4	+7.7	+2.7	−25.0	−21.0	avg	avg	+0.13	−0.24	1.80	9.0
Univ Svgs American		12/78	Mackenzie Finl. (9 yrs.)	48.6	9.29	n.a.	+13.7	+13.0	−5.5	−14.1	avg	avg	+0.23	−0.05	2.00	9.0
Viking Growth		03/49	Multiple	125.7	16.34	+15.4	+14.3	+15.1	−10.4	−15.0	avg −	avg	+0.27	−0.12	1.69	(f)
			Average:	49.0		+14.5	+8.8	+8.0	−14.6	−21.6	64.64	97.11	+0.14	−0.14		

Fund name	RRSP & RRIF eligible	Launch date	Fund manager (Years)	Total net assets $ millions Mar.31, 1988	Net asset value per share	Average annual compound rate of return ‡ 10 yr. %	5 yr.	3 yr.	Simple rates of return 1 yr. %	6 mo.	Variability 5 yr.	1 yr.	Reward/risk ratio 5 yr.	1 yr.	Expense ratio %	Maximum sales redempt. charge %
INTERNATIONAL EQUITY FUNDS																
AGF Hi-Tech		06/83	K. J. Whiting	11.3	13.16	n.a.	n.a.	+15.2	−2.2	−13.6	n.a.	avg	n.a.	−0.02	2.11	9.0
AGF Option		04/79	R.D. Cameron	26.5	3.67	n.a.	+5.5	+2.2	−11.3	−15.5	avg −	avg −	+0.13	−0.18	1.64	9.0
Allied International		12/85	Robin McIsaac (2 yrs)	4.9	4.66	n.a.	n.a.	n.a.	−31.9	−38.5	n.a.	avg +	n.a.	−0.26	2.00	nil
B Tremblay Int'l		03/61	P. Spark	444.2	6.74	+19.6	+15.0	+14.0	−10.1	−20.5	avg +	avg	+0.19	−0.11	1.84	9.0
Dynamic Global		10/86	Beutel Goodman	22.2	5.09	n.a.	n.a.	n.a.	−3.6	−15.0	n.a.	avg −	n.a.	−0.04	2.00	9.0
Fonds Desjard Intl		12/59		9.9	13.42	+12.1	+9.0	+10.1	−14.2	−24.1	avg	avg	+0.14	−0.17	n.a.	nil
Global Strategy Americas		01/87	Worldwide Financial Ltd.	5.2	8.96	n.a.	n.a.	n.a.	−16.8	−24.3	n.a.	avg	n.a.	−0.16	1.93	9.0
Global Strategy Corp.	R	09/85	Worldwide Capital Mgmt	9.7	16.71	n.a.	n.a.	n.a.	−9.0	−19.8	n.a.	avg	n.a.	−0.10	2.93	nil
Global Strategy Europe		01/87	Worldwide Financial Ltd.	4.6	8.24	n.a.	n.a.	n.a.	−17.6	−23.7	n.a.	avg	n.a.	−0.21	1.79	9.0
Global Strategy Far East		01/87	Worldwide Financial Ltd.	21.0	10.72	n.a.	n.a.	n.a.	+5.0	−14.6	n.a.	avg +	n.a.	+0.04	1.73	9.0
Global Strategy Fund		08/85	Worldwide Capital Mgmt	254.9	13.89	n.a.	n.a.	n.a.	−9.3	−19.2	n.a.	avg	n.a.	−0.10	2.14	9.0
Guardian World Equity		08/71	Marathon Asset Mgt.(1 yr)	23.4	3.90	+16.6	+13.2	+15.0	−9.1	−17.8	avg	avg	+0.23	−0.10	1.11	9.0
Industrial Global		09/85	Mackenzie Financial Corp.	243.2	6.09	n.a.	n.a.	n.a.	+6.1	−8.0	n.a.	avg	n.a.	+0.07	n.a.	9.0
International Growth		02/66	Stephen Raphael(2 yrs)	2.8	7.96	+14.1	+12.0	+11.0	−5.9	−18.5	avg	avg	+0.19	−0.06	1.82	9.0
Investors Global Fund		10/86	I.G. Invest. Mgmt. Ltd.	228.6	5.14	n.a.	n.a.	n.a.	−7.4	−18.6	n.a.	avg	n.a.	−0.09	1.56	8.5
MD Growth Investments		07/69	MD Management Ltd.	754.3	16.35	+22.5	+19.6	+18.9	−4.7	−17.7	avg	avg +	+0.31	−0.04	0.80	(q)
MER Growth		02/83	Merritt Easton Rae(4 yrs)	0.2	7.90	n.a.	+4.5	−0.9	−13.5	−23.7	avg	avg +	+0.07	−0.12	4.06	8.5
Montreal Trust Int'l	U	12/64	Montrusco Associates Inc.	18.2	17.63	+15.5	+13.5	+17.1	−9.9	−17.6	avg	avg	+0.22	−0.10	1.59	nil
Morgan Worldwide		02/84	John Zechner (Incep)	6.8 (c)	13.15	n.a.	n.a.	+5.6	−17.8	−25.5	n.a.	avg	n.a.	−0.21	1.95	9.0
Saxon World Growth		12/85	Robert Tattersall (Incep)	3.4	10.59	n.a.	n.a.	n.a.	−5.9	−19.6	n.a.	avg +	n.a.	−0.05	1.75	nil
Sceptre International		11/86	Sceptre Invest Couns.	1.0	9.79	n.a.	n.a.	n.a.	−12.1	−23.0	n.a.	avg	n.a.	−0.12	2.18	nil
Sentinel Global		09/86	Sentinel Invest. Mgmt.	89.4	8.64	n.a.	n.a.	n.a.	−14.1	−25.7	n.a.	avg +	n.a.	−0.13	2.58	5.0
Templeton Growth		11/54	Templeton Invest. Coun.	1,284.7	17.11	+17.3	+15.3	+13.0	−9.5	−19.7	avg	avg	+0.28	−0.10	0.73	8.5
Trimark		09/81	Trimark Invest Mgmt.	555.4	10.39	n.a.	+14.5	+13.9	−3.8	−15.5	avg	avg	+0.23	−0.03	1.59	9.0
United Accumulative		05/57	Gerald Coleman (9 yrs)	241.3	9.82	+18.7	+14.1	+9.0	−13.2	−17.9	avg	avg	+0.27	−0.15	1.70	9.0
Universal Savings Global		06/86	Universal Svgs. Mgmt. 1yr.	43.5	5.08	n.a.	n.a.	n.a.	−4.3	−15.8	n.a.	avg	n.a.	−0.05	2.00	9.0
Universal Savings Pacific		12/81	Universal Svgs.Mgt(5 yrs)	32.4	8.98	n.a.	+28.8	+37.1	+9.9	−8.7	avg +	avg +	+0.38	+0.09	2.00	9.0
Viking Commonwealth		04/32	Multiple	168.8	13.38	+16.0	+15.7	+16.0	−0.4	−9.4	avg −	avg −	+0.37	−0.00	1.65	(f)
Viking International		04/68	Multiple	136.5	17.73	+16.7	+13.8	+10.8	−4.2	−13.7	avg	avg	+0.25	−0.04	1.64	(f)
Walwyn Int'l		12/85	Stephen Raphael (2 yrs)	5.9	10.18	n.a.	n.a.	n.a.	−9.3	−20.0	n.a.	avg	n.a.	−0.10	2.88	5.0
Walwyn Option Equity		12/85	Robert McLeish (2 yrs)	3.2	9.02	n.a.	n.a.	n.a.	−3.5	−10.5	n.a.	avg	n.a.	−0.03	2.04	5.0
			Average:	150.2		+16.9	+13.9	+13.0	−8.2	−18.6	58.62	91.60	+0.23	−0.09		

Fund name	RRSP & RRIF eligible	Launch date	Fund manager (Years)	Total net assets $ millions Mar.31, 1988	Net asset value per share Mar.31, 1988	Average annual compound rate of return ‡ 10 yr. %	5 yr. %	3 yr. %	Simple rates of return 1 yr. %	6 mo. %	Variability 5 yr.	1 yr.	Reward/risk ratio 5 yr.	1 yr.	Expense ratio %	Maximum sales redempt. charge %

FUNDS LAUNCHED IN PAST YEAR

Fund name	RRSP & RRIF eligible	Launch date	Fund manager (Years)	Total net assets $ millions Mar.31, 1988	Net asset value per share Mar.31, 1988	Change since int. offering date	Maximum Sales redempt. charge %
CANADIAN EQUITY FUNDS							
B Tremblay Discovery	R	10/87	John Sartz (6 mos.)	5.0	5.19	+4.8	9.0
CIBC Global Equity		01/88	CIBC Invest. Mgmt.(incep)	10.3	10.12	+1.2	nil
Central's Cdn Growth	R	09/87	Central Trust Co.	16.3	10.26	+3.5	nil
Fidelity Intl. Portfolio		01/88	Fidelity Intl Invest Ltd	3.1	9.71	+2.2	
Global Strategy RRSP	R	12/87	Worldwide Capital Mgmt.	1.9	9.04	−0.6	9.0
Global Strategy RRSP Access	R	01/88	Worldwide Capital Mgmt.	1.4	9.96	−0.3	4.2
Hume Canadian Equity	R	01/88	Hume Fund Mgmt. Inc.	0.6	10.10	+1.4	nil
Industrial Future Fund	R	12/87	Mackenzie Invest. Mgrs.	37.4	5.16	+3.2	5.0
NFM Canadian Equity	R	11/87	Nthn. Investors Inc.	0.3	5.27	+6.1	9.0
Perpetual Growth Fund II ...		04/87	M D Management	34.2	7.73	−17.1	nil
St-Laurent Placmt. Actions		01/88	Carmand Normand	0.5	9.87	−1.2	4.0
Universal Sector Canadian .		11/87	Mackenzie Financial Corp.	3.8	5.51	+10.2	9.0
FIXED INCOME FUNDS							
B Tremblay Bond & Mtge ..	R	11/87	Pierre Garceau (6 mos.)	9.3	5.03	+1.1	5.0
CIBC Fixed Income	R	12/87	CIBC Invest. Mgmt.(Incep)	10.5	10.05	+0.5	nil
Central's Gov't Bond	R	09/87	Central Trust Co.	7.4	10.30	+5.5	nil
Guardian Strategic Income	R	05/87	Larry T. Kennedy (Incep.)	12.9	10.07	+5.6	5.0
Hume Canadian Bond	R	11/87	Hume Fund Mgmt. Inc.	1.7	10.16	+1.7	
Noram Cdn Convertible Sec	R	01/88	Andrew Willman (Incep)	10.0	10.19	+1.9	9.0
St-Laurent Placmt. Oblig. ..		01/88	Carmand Normand	0.6	10.01	+0.1	4.0
BALANCED FUNDS							
B Tremblay Cdn Balanced ..	R	01/88	Jean Luc Landry	3.6	5.08	+1.8	9.0
CIBC Bal Inc & Growth	R	12/87	CIBC Invest. Mgmt.(Incep)	12.3	10.48	+4.9	nil
Central's Select	R	09/87	Central Trust Co.	6.0	10.26	+4.3	nil
Fidelity Capital Balanced ...	R	02/88	Fidelity Intl Invest Ltd	0.6	10.33	+3.3	4.0
Fidelity Capital Builder	R	02/88	Fidelity Intl Invest Ltd	0.6	10.65	+6.5	4.0
Fidelity Capital Conservation	R	02/88	Fidelity Intl Invest Ltd	0.4	10.00	—0.0	4.0
Integra Balanced	R	01/88	Gryphon Inv. Counsel	2.7	10.23	+2.3	5.0
Royfund Balanced	R	12/87		25.3	5.11	+2.6	nil
Sunset World	R	07/87	Connor, Clark & Lunn	110.0	9.67	+0.2	9.0
Trimark Income Growth ...		09/87	Trimark Invest. Mgmt.	15.9	5.13	+4.3	9.0
DIVIDEND FUNDS							
Central's Income		09/87	Central Trust Co.	2.4	10.29	+3.3	nil
Fonds SNF Revenu	R	01/88	Placement SNF Inc.	1.0	10.04	—0.0	6.5

Fund name	RRSP & RRIF eligible	Launch date	Fund manager (Years)	Total net assets $ millions	Net asset value per share Mar.31, 1988	Average annual compound rate of return ‡ 10 yr.	5 yr. (%)	3 yr.	Simple rates of return 1 yr.	6 mo. (%)	Variability 5 yr.	1 yr.	Reward/risk ratio 5 yr.	1 yr.	Expense ratio %	Maximum sales redempt. charge %
REAL ESTATE FUNDS																
Pagebrook Realty A	R	09/87	Roycom Securities Ltd.						3.4		9.20		—0.0	2.0		
Pagebrook Realty B		09/87	Roycom Securities Ltd.						4.6		9.50		—0.0	2.0		
PRECIOUS METAL FUNDS																
Universal Sector Resource		11/87	MacKenzie Financial Corp.						3.1		5.62		+12.4	9.0		
U.S. EQUITY FUNDS																
NFM U.S. Equity	U	11/87	Nthn. Investors Inc.						0.1		4.97		+0.2	9.0		
Sentinel Amer. Equity		07/87	Sentinel Invest. Mgmt.						41.0		8.21		−13.6	5.0		
Universal Sector American .		11/87	MacKenzie Financial Corp.						10.3		5.38		+7.6	9.0		
INTERNATIONAL EQUITY FUNDS																
BPI Europe & Far East	R	06/87	Kleinwort Grieveson Inv.						3.3		8.20		−13.7	9.0		
G.T. Global Choice		11/87	G.T. Management						0.9		5.28		+18.8	9.0		
Royal Tr Global Invest		07/87	Corp. Invest. Assoc.						7.5		7.95		−20.2	nil		
Universal Sector Global		11/87	Universal Savings Mgmt.						6.6		5.11		+2.2	9.0		
Universal Sector Pacific . . .		11/87	Universal Savings Mgmt.						2.4		5.64		+12.8	9.0		
MONEY MARKET FUNDS																
AMD Canadian T-Bill		09/87	Midland Doherty (Incep.)						279.3		10.00		+4.7	1.0		
Global Strategy Govt Money	R	12/87	Worldwide Capital Mgmt.						1.2		1.00		—0.0	nil		
Global Strategy World Money	R	12/87	Worldwide Capital Mgmt.						3.3		9.65		+0.8	4.0		
Montreal Trust Investment . .		10/87	Montrusco Associates						10.7		10.00		+3.4	nil		
Montreal Trust Registered . .	R	07/87	Montrusco Associates						16.1		10.00		+5.4	nil		
Royal Tr Cdn Money Mkt . . .	R	07/87	Corp. Invest. Assoc.						273.0		10.00		+5.3	nil		
Sceptre Money Market	R	11/87	Sceptre Invest. Counsel						10.4		10.00		+1.6	nil		
St-Laurent Placmt-Monetaire		01/88	Carmand Normand						0.6		9.99		−0.1	4.0		
United Cdn. Money Market	R	01/88	United Finl. Mgmt. Ltd.						7.7		10.00		—0.0	2.0		
Waltaine Instant $$		08/87	Hodgson Roberton Laing						1.8		10.06		+3.9	nil		
U.S. MONEY MARKET FUNDS																
Global Strategy US Money .	U	12/87	Worldwide Capital Mgmt.						0.5		1.00		—0.0	nil		
United U.S.Dollar Money Mkt		01/88	United Finl. Mgmt. Ltd.						6.3		5.00		—0.0	2.0		
INTERNATIONAL MONEY MARKET FUNDS																
NFM Intl Money Mkt & Inc . .		11/87	Nthn. Investors Inc.						0.2		5.09		+3.4	2.0		
Universal Sector Currency . .		11/87	Universal Savings Mgmt.						0.8		5.07		+1.4	9.0		

Life Insurance Funds

Fund name	RRSP & RRIF eligible	Launch date	Fund manager (Years)	Total net assets $ millions	Net asset value per share Mar.31, 1988	Average annual compound rate of return ‡ 10 yr. %	5 yr. %	3 yr. %	Simple rates of return 1 yr. %	6 mo. %	Variability 5 yr.	1 yr.	Reward/risk ratio 5 yr.	1 yr.	Expense ratio %	Maximum sales redempt. charge %
CANADIAN EQUITY FUNDS																
Canada Life E.2	R	11/62	Can. Life Inv Mgt (3 yrs)	7.7	153.44	+17.4	+15.3	+13.8	−7.5	−10.9	avg	avg	+0.26	−0.08	1.00	
Canada Life S.9	R	08/69	Can. Life Inv Mgt (3 yrs)	171.5	70.65	+16.5	+14.2	+12.7	−6.2	−8.1	avg	avg −	+0.27	−0.07	2.00	
Canadian Equity 2	R	12/69		18.3	6.24	+14.6	+9.7	+8.4	−14.5	−18.3	avg	avg +	+0.16	−0.14	n.a.	
Cdn General Life A	R	06/68	Guaranty Tr. Co.	3.4	117.45	+17.8	+14.1	+11.4	−9.7	−13.0	avg	avg	+0.23	−0.10	1.38	
Canadian Reassurance ..		06/69	M. Corbett (15 yrs)	0.8	75.47	+17.0	+13.4	+12.7	−11.7	−15.5	avg	avg	+0.23	−0.13	n.a.	
Citadel Life	R	07/70	Patty Stewart (1 yr)	5.1	8.78	+16.2	+10.4	+10.1	−10.2	−13.2	avg	avg +	+0.17	−0.09	0.77	
Confed Life A		01/69	Confederation Life	n.a.	12.05	+16.3	+14.2	+11.2	−6.7	−7.1	avg −	avg	+0.28	−0.08	0.48	
Confed Life B	R	01/69	Confederation Life	n.a.	11.36	+16.1	+14.1	+11.7	−4.2	−6.4	avg −	avg −	+0.28	−0.05	0.96	
Crown Life (CCIFA)	R	07/68	Beutel, Goodman & Co. Ltd	33.4	56.38	+13.6	+14.9	+18.1	−5.9	−11.0	avg	avg	+0.26	−0.06	n.a.	
Crown Life Commitment ..	R	11/87	Beutel Goodman (1 yr.)	n.a.	16.33	n.a.	n.a.	n.a.	−5.7	−9.9	n.a.	avg	n.a.	−0.06	1.00	
Crown Life Equity	R	11/87	Beutel,Goodman(2 1/2 yrs)	n.a.	79.89	+13.4	+13.4	+15.5	−5.1	−10.0	avg	avg	+0.25	−0.06	0.70	
Crown Life Foreign Equity		11/87	Beutel,Goodman(2 1/2 yrs)	n.a.	37.56	n.a.	+13.2	+12.8	−1.9	−13.6	avg	avg −	+0.22	−0.02	0.70	
L'Assur-Vie Desjard Stock		01/66		13.4	78.85	+17.3	+12.9	+13.4	−15.1	−17.5	avg	avg	+0.23	−0.17	n.a.	
Empire Life Fund 3	R	01/71	Donald Miano (2 yrs.)	33.5	11.47	+21.3	+14.9	+16.9	−5.8	−5.6	avg	avg −	+0.26	−0.07	1.20	
Empire Life Fund 1	R	64	Donald Miano (12 yrs)	133.9	43.03	+19.2	+13.0	+14.3	−3.2	−8.3	avg	avg	+0.23	−0.03	1.20	
Empire Life Fund 5	R	12/69	Donald Miano (12 yrs)	2.0	55.28	+20.5	+13.7	+11.1	−16.9	−19.9	avg +	avg +	+0.21	−0.16	0.50	
Equitable Life Canada ...	R	07/66	Ian Lee (1 yr.)	15.7	8.23	+15.3	+11.6	+11.3	−14.8	−18.7	avg +	avg +	+0.17	−0.14	1.04	
Impco Growth		02/69	Imperial Life	n.a.	70.47	+15.7	+12.1	+11.5	−12.1	−21.4	avg +	avg +	+0.19	−0.11	n.a.	
Impco Ret Growth	R	03/69	Imperial Life	n.a.	97.50	+19.8	+19.3	+22.6	+5.8	−7.0	avg +	avg +	+0.30	+0.05	n.a.	
London Life Equity	R	12/61	Rohit Sehgal (6 yrs)	142.3	120.01	+17.2	+13.4	+12.6	−7.0	−12.4	avg	avg	+0.24	−0.08	0.98	
Manufacturers Cap Gains	R	01/84	Manuvest (Incep)	25.0	1.46	n.a.	n.a.	+10.5	−11.5	−16.4	n.a.	avg +	n.a.	−0.11	n.a.	
Manufacturers Equity	R	12/70	Manuvest (Incep)	181.1	6.12	+15.2	+8.5	+7.6	−9.7	−15.0	avg	avg	+0.14	−0.10	n.a.	
Maritime Life Growth	R	06/85	Maritime Life	143.2	12.53	n.a.	n.a.	n.a.	−11.4	−16.0	n.a.	avg	n.a.	−0.12	n.a.	
MONY Canadian Growth .	R	07/74	Tor. Invest. Mgmt.(Incep)	123.9	55.11	+16.4	+9.8	+8.2	−21.6	−16.6	avg −	avg	+0.19	−0.26	2.00	
Mutual Life A	R	03/62	Mucana Investment (Incep)	118.7	97.37	+15.6	+10.6	+7.0	−11.7	−13.2	avg	avg	+0.18	−0.12	n.a.	
Mutual Life B	R	11/71	Mucana Investment (Incep)	12.9	67.82	+17.8	+12.9	+9.8	−9.6	−11.0	avg	avg +	+0.21	−0.09	n.a.	
Nat'l Life Equities	R	05/61	Jim Blake (9 yrs)	18.7	156.47	+16.7	+13.9	+12.5	−4.8	−11.8	avg	avg	+0.24	−0.05	n.a.	
Nat'l Life of Cda	R	10/71	Jim Blake (9 yrs)	0.7	62.74	+16.2	+13.9	+11.8	−7.5	−13.3	avg	avg	+0.24	−0.08	n.a.	
Sovereign Growth Equity .	R	01/86	Bissett & Assoc.	3.5	10.25	n.a.	n.a.	n.a.	−13.9	−12.7	n.a.	avg	n.a.	−0.16	2.00	
Standard EQUIfund	R	02/87	Standard Life Assur. Co.	8.4	10.15	n.a.	n.a.	n.a.	−12.9	−16.6	n.a.	avg	n.a.	−0.14	0.40	
Sunfund	R	04/69	Sunimco	89.7	55.78	+15.7	+12.7	+11.2	−4.4	−7.8	avg −	avg −	+0.25	−0.06	1.00	
			Average:	54.5		+16.8	+13.1	+12.2	−8.9	−12.8	56.71	89.50	+0.23	−0.09		

Fund name	RRSP & RRIF eligible	Launch date	Fund manager (Years)	Total net assets $ millions Mar.31, 1988	Net asset value per share	Average annual compound rate of return ‡ 10 yr. %	5 yr. %	3 yr. %	Simple rates of return 1 yr. %	6 mo. %	Variability 5 yr.	Variability 1 yr.	Reward/risk ratio 5 yr.	Reward/risk ratio 1 yr.	Expense ratio %	Maximum sales redempt. charge %
FIXED INCOME FUNDS																
Canada Life S.19	R	10/73	Can. Life Inv Mgt (3 yrs)	37.8	40.42	+10.5	+11.5	+11.2	+2.7	+9.0	avg	avg	+0.54	+0.09	2.00	
Cdn General Life B	R	03/69	Guaranty Tr. Co.	2.0	62.95	+12.5	+10.6	+9.5	−1.3	+3.0	avg	avg	+0.50	−0.07	1.27	
Confed Life C	R	12/70	Confederation Life	n.a.	6.98	+13.9	+17.7	+15.2	+7.5	+14.0	avg +	avg +	+0.57	+0.13	1.44	
Crown Life Bond	R	11/87	P.V. Tuters (8 mos)	103.7	322.20	+8.0	+8.1	+9.3	+3.5	+10.2	avg	avg	+0.32	+0.11	n.a.	
Crown Life Mortgage	R	11/87	N.A.G. Howard (4 yrs)	42.4	854.36	+11.4	+12.5	+12.8	+6.4	+8.4	avg −	avg −	+0.90	+0.42	1.20	
L'Assur-Vie Desjard Bond		01/66		14.7	62.49	+11.6	+13.8	+13.4	+3.4	+11.4	avg	avg	+0.56	+0.09	n.a.	
L'Assur-Vie Desjard Mtge		01/72		11.8	50.54	+11.7	+12.3	+12.7	+7.7	+7.9	avg −	avg −	+1.12	+0.68	n.a.	
Empire Life Fund 2	R	03/86	Paul Pugh (2 yrs)	3.2	11.07	n.a.	n.a.	n.a.	−0.6	+7.5	n.a.	avg	n.a.	−0.02	1.20	
Equit Life Cda Bd Mtge ..	R	11/69	Ian Lee (11 yrs)	10.4	5.81	+11.4	+12.7	+13.0	+5.1	+9.3	avg	avg	+0.65	+0.21	1.56	
London Life Bond	R	12/61	Charles Hughson (4 yrs)	217.1	78.22	+12.1	+14.2	+14.3	−2.9	+9.0	avg +	avg +	+0.38	−0.05	0.98	
London Life Mortgage ...	R	07/69	Doug Campbell (2 yrs)	77.2	57.03	+10.7	+12.0	+12.7	+6.6	+5.9	avg	avg −	+0.77	+0.79	1.34	
Manufacturers Bond	R	01/84	Manuvest (Incep)	27.9	1.59	n.a.	n.a.	+12.5	+4.1	+11.3	n.a.	avg	n.a.	+0.10	n.a.	
MONY Bond	R	12/86	Laketon Invest. Mgt.	8.6	9.38	n.a.	n.a.	n.a.	−0.6	+10.4	n.a.	avg +	n.a.	−0.01	2.00	
Mutual Life 2..........	R	06/74	Mucana Investment (Incep)	8.3	48.52	+12.3	+13.4	+14.6	+5.1	+10.3	avg	avg	+0.59	+0.17	n.a.	
Nat'l Life Fixed	R	12/62	Nang Cheung (3 yrs)	3.0	77.82	+12.4	+14.0	+14.0	+5.0	+11.0	avg	avg	+0.58	+0.16	n.a.	
Seaboard Life Accum 2 ..	R	01/68	Bob Farley (11 mos)	2.9	4.76	n.a.	+10.1	+11.1	+4.7	+7.0	avg	avg	+0.54	+0.28	1.50	
Sovereign Cap Sec Bond	R	01/86	Bissett & Assoc.	457.8	11.17	n.a.	n.a.	n.a.	+4.3	+9.2	n.a.	avg	n.a.	+0.17	2.00	
Standard BONDfund	R	02/87	Standard Life Assur. Co.	2.7	10.97	n.a.	n.a.	n.a.	+5.5	+12.4	n.a.	avg	n.a.	+0.13	0.40	
			Average:	60.7		+11.5	+12.5	+12.6	+3.7	+9.3	21.91	29.56	+0.62	+0.19		
BALANCED FUNDS																
Canada Life S.35	R	03/84	Can. Life Invest Mgmt	310.4	16.77	n.a.	n.a.	+12.5	−2.0	−1.4	n.a.	avg	n.a.	−0.04	2.00	
Crown Life Balanced	R	11/87	Beutel Goodman(1 1/2 yrs)	n.a.	120.41	n.a.	n.a.	n.a.	−0.0	+0.8	n.a.	avg	n.a.	−0.00	1.50	
Manufacturers Diversified	R	01/81	Manuvest (Incep)	398.9	46.85	n.a.	+10.4	+11.1	−4.1	−4.9	avg	avg +	+0.10	−0.08	n.a.	
Maritime Life Balanced ..	R	08/86	Maritime Life	37.3	10.74	n.a.	n.a.	n.a.	−3.3	−1.2	n.a.	avg	n.a.	−0.10	n.a.	
NAL Investor Blue Chip ..	R	04/87	Elliott & Page	4.2	9.31	n.a.	n.a.	n.a.	n.a.	−14.5	n.a.	n.a.	n.a.	n.a.	n.a.	
NAL Investor Diversified ..	R	04/87	Elliott & Page	4.6	10.09	n.a.	n.a.	n.a.	n.a.	−1.9	n.a.	n.a.	n.a.	n.a.	n.a.	
Sovereign Revenue Growth	R	01/86	Bisset & Assoc.	1.3	11.23	n.a.	n.a.	n.a.	+2.1	+4.6	n.a.	avg −	n.a.	+0.11	2.00	
Standard DIVERSIfund ...	R	02/87	Standard Life Assur. Co.	7.5	10.56	n.a.	n.a.	n.a.	−3.5	−2.3	n.a.	avg	n.a.	−0.09	0.40	
Transamerica B.I.G.	R	02/79	Larry Kennedy (9 yrs.)	36.1	12.48	n.a.	+10.8	+8.8	+5.6	+1.5	avg	avg −	+0.53	+0.42	1.80	
			Average:	100.0		n.a.	+10.6	+10.8	−0.9	−2.1	58.74	31.19	+0.32	+0.04		
MONEY MARKET FUNDS																
Canada Life S.29	R	10/74	Can. Life Inv Mgt (3 yrs)	50.0	34.90	+10.5	+8.1	+7.2	+6.6	+3.6	avg	avg	+2.51	+4.28	2.00	
Cdn. General Life C	R	12/86	Guaranty Tr. Co.	0.1	10.83	n.a.	n.a.	n.a.	+6.7	+3.3	n.a.	avg	n.a.	+2.87	0.92	
Crown Life Short Term ...	R	11/87	Beutel Goodman(2 1/2 yrs)	73.6	203.96	n.a.	+9.3	+9.1	+8.3	+5.0	avg	avg +	+4.44	+2.72	0.52	
Manufacturers Short Term	R	01/84	Manuvest (Incep)	47.8	1.45	n.a.	n.a.	+8.9	+8.0	+4.5	n.a.	avg	n.a.	+2.96	n.a.	
MONY T-Bill	R	12/86	MONY Capital Mgmt	2.8	1.00	n.a.	n.a.	n.a.	+6.6	+3.3	n.a.	avg −	n.a.	+14.34	2.00	
			Average:	34.9		+10.5	+8.7	+8.4	+7.2	+3.9	2.66	2.02	+3.48	+5.43		

Life Insurance Funds

Fund name	RRSP & RRIF eligible	Launch date	Fund manager (Years)	Total net assets $ millions Mar.31, 1988	Net asset value per share Mar.31, 1988	Average annual compound rate of return ‡ 10 yr. %	5 yr. %	3 yr. %	Simple rates of return 1 yr. %	6 mo. %	Variability 5 yr.	Variability 1 yr.	Reward/risk ratio 5 yr.	Reward/risk ratio 1 yr.	Expense ratio %	Maximum sales redempt. charge %
REAL ESTATE FUNDS																
Sovereign Save & Prosper	R	01/82	Sovereign Life	25.3	12.82	n.a.	+4.1	+3.2	+7.8	+5.8	avg	avg	+0.20	+0.88	2.00	
			Average:	25.3		n.a.	+4.1	+3.2	+7.8	+5.8	20.01	8.81	+0.20	+0.88		
U.S. EQUITY FUNDS																
Canada Life S34		01/86	Can. Life Inv Mgt (Incep)	30.2	16.75	n.a.	n.a.	n.a.	−6.7	−11.9	n.a.	avg −	n.a.	−0.09	2.00	
Fidelity Life Growth		10/69	Bob Farley (10 mos)	1.1	53.07	+14.6	+9.5	+8.3	−1.7	−10.2	avg +	avg	+0.16	−0.01	0.50	
Seaboard Life Accum 1 ..		01/68	Bob Farley (11 mos)	2.5	4.32	n.a.	+9.7	+8.1	−5.2	−11.1	avg	avg	+0.17	−0.06	1.50	
			Average:	11.3		+14.6	+9.6	+8.2	−4.5	−11.1	56.13	81.63	+0.17	−0.05		

FUNDS LAUNCHED IN PAST YEAR

Fund name	RRSP & RRIF eligible	Launch date	Fund manager (Years)	Total net assets $ millions Mar.31, 1988	Net asset value per share Mar.31, 1988	Change since int. offering date	Maximum Sales redempt. charge %
FIXED INCOME FUNDS							
NAL Investor Bond	R	05/87	Elliott & Page	1.7	10.63	+6.4	
Spectrum Interest	R	07/87	Sunimco (Incep.)	24.7	9.86	+5.2	
BALANCED FUNDS							
London Life Diversified	R	01/88	R. Bruce McCarthy (4 yrs)	9.7	62.01	+3.4	
MONY Balanced	R	04/87	E.J. McConnell & Assoc.	4.6	9.26	−2.1	
Spectrum Diversified	R	07/87	Sunimco	26.1	9.82	+0.2	
DIVIDEND FUNDS							
Spectrum Dividend	R	07/87	Sunimco (Incep.)	6.8	9.59	+0.7	
MONEY MARKET FUNDS							
Spectrum Cash Reserve ...	R	07/87	Sunimco (Incep.)	12.6	1.00	+6.6	
Spectrum Savings		08/87	Sunimco (Incep.)	11.7	1.00	+5.4	
CANADIAN EQUITY FUNDS							
Mutual Cdn. Indexfund	R	11/87	Mu-Cana Invest. Couns.	2.8	8.32	+12.1	
Spectrum Cdn. Equity	R	07/87	Sunimco (Incep.)	15.1	9.41	−5.1	
U.S. EQUITY FUNDS							
London Life U.S. Equity ...	R	01/88	Tim Burt (1 3/4 yrs.)	5.4	9.86	—0.0	
INTERNATIONAL EQUITY FUNDS							
MONY Global		04/87	Martin Currie Inc.	4.8	8.47	−15.3	
Spectrum Intl. Equity		07/87	Sunimco (Incep.)	5.3	8.23	−17.2	

Market Benchmarks

	Value Mar.31, 1988	Average annual compound rate of return (%) ‡ 10 yr.	5 yr.	3 yr.	Simple rate of return (%) 1 yr.	6 mo.	Variability 5 yr.	1 yr.	Reward/risk ratio 5 yr.	1 yr.
TSE Total Return Index	5,166.26	+16.5	+12.6	+11.6	−8.8	−13.7	+59.28	+93.61	+0.21	−0.09
Standard & Poor's 500 Stocks .	258.89	+11.2	+11.1	+12.7	−11.2	−19.6	+62.51	+96.08	+0.17	−0.11
Nikkei - Dow Jones..........	26,320.00	n.a.	+25.4	+27.9	+18.7	+1.2	+54.57	+67.33	+0.46	+0.27
World Capital Index..........	449.90	n.a.	+22.1	+30.5	+3.3	−7.3	+51.40	+75.56	+0.42	+0.04
Gold Bullion - London P.M. Fix . .	$456.95	+9.7	+2.0	+11.5	+8.5	−0.6	+52.86	+55.51	+0.03	+0.15
Morguard Property Index(m) . . .	929.80	+13.2	+12.1	+13.6	+14.2	+7.3	+18.79	+20.10	+0.64	+0.70
3 Month Treasury Bills	8.81%	+10.9	+9.6	+9.2	+8.5	+2.8	+6.50	+7.41	+1.47	+1.14
6 Month Treasury Bills	8.54%	+11.1	+9.9	+9.5	+8.9	+2.9	+6.85	+6.60	+1.44	+1.34
MYW long-term Corporate Bonds	10.76%	+12.6	+12.0	+11.5	+10.8	+3.3	+2.96	+3.52	+4.05	+3.06

(m) MPI measures the performance of Canadian real estate as a class and does not reflect the performance of real estate managed by Morguard Investments Ltd.

March 31, 1988
Mutual Funds Performance (All Categories)
5 years †

Fund name	RRSP & RRIF eligible	Launch date	Fund manager (Years)	Total net assets $ millions Mar.31, 1988	Net asset value per share Mar.31, 1988	Average annual compound rate of return ‡ 10 yr. %	5 yr. %	3 yr. %	Simple rates of return 1 yr. %	6 mo. %	Variability 5 yr.	1 yr.	Reward/risk ratio 5 yr.	1 yr.	Expense ratio %	Maximum sales redempt. charge %
Mutual Funds - All Categories																
AGF Japan		01/69	R.J. Whiting	105.3	6.55	+23.5	+35.2	+42.5	+28.9	+2.3	avg +	avg +	+0.52	+0.30	1.56	9.0
Investors Japanese		03/71	I.G. Invest. Mgmt. Ltd.	194.6	16.47	+21.6	+32.2	+41.1	+32.3	+10.4	avg	avg −	+0.49	+0.50	1.32	8.5
Universal Savings Pacific		12/81	Universal Svgs.Mgt(5 yrs)	32.4	8.98	n.a.	+28.8	+37.1	+9.9	−8.7	avg +	avg +	+0.38	+0.09	2.00	9.0
Trans-Canada Equity	R	01/72	Sagit Management	4.6	7.30	+16.5	+23.5	+24.5	−0.2	−1.1	avg	avg	+0.48	−0.00	2.00	8.75
Cambridge Growth	R	08/66	Sagit Management Ltd.	1.4	6.66	+16.6	+21.9	+22.6	−0.8	−3.5	avg	avg	+0.44	−0.01	2.00	8.75
MD Growth Investments		07/69	MD Management Ltd.	754.3	16.35	+22.5	+19.6	+18.9	−4.7	−17.7	avg	avg +	+0.31	−0.04	0.80	(q)
Trans-Cda Shares B		09/44	Sagit Management Ltd.	0.9	76.74	+15.5	+18.1	+21.4	+5.3	+5.8	avg −	avg −	+0.52	+0.10	1.94	(e)
Industrial Dividend	R	12/77	Mackenzie Invest. Mgrs.	269.4	10.82	+16.8	+17.5	+16.9	−0.7	−9.3	avg	avg	+0.31	−0.00	n.a.	9.0
Trans-Cda Shares C	R	12/50	Sagit Management	6.8	12.83	+14.3	+16.6	+18.9	+1.3	+2.4	avg −	avg −	+0.39	+0.02	1.92	(e)
Universal Savings Eq	R	04/65	Mackenzie Finl. (13 yrs)	118.3	10.95	+18.0	+16.4	+17.8	+3.6	−2.4	avg	avg	+0.32	+0.04	2.00	9.0
CMA Investment	R	03/66	MD Management Ltd.	863.3	28.62	+17.8	+16.3	+16.3	+3.0	−3.6	avg −	avg	+0.39	+0.04	0.75	(q)
Industrial Pension	R	02/71	Mackenzie Invest. Mgrs.	142.9	5.99	+16.0	+15.8	+16.1	−3.0	−10.0	avg	avg	+0.27	−0.03	n.a.	9.0
Industrial Income	R	07/74	Mackenzie Invest. Mgrs.	117.0	10.00	+11.5	+15.8	+17.4	+11.2	+6.5	avg	avg	+0.68	+0.61	n.a.	9.0
Mackenzie Equity	R	05/73	Mackenzie Invest. Mgrs.	70.0	2.42	+19.5	+15.7	+16.7	−1.7	−8.7	avg	avg	+0.28	−0.01	n.a.	9.0
Royfund Equity	R	12/66	Martin Siegerman (15 yrs)	852.8	20.18	+18.4	+15.7	+13.6	−10.5	−13.4	avg	avg	+0.30	−0.13	0.51	nil
Viking Commonwealth		04/32	Multiple	168.8	13.38	+16.0	+15.7	+16.0	−0.4	−9.4	avg −	avg −	+0.37	−0.00	1.65	(f)
Industrial Growth	R	10/67	Mackenzie Invest. Mgrs.	1,615.3	14.64	+17.8	+15.6	+16.0	+1.5	−6.7	avg	avg	+0.32	+0.01	n.a.	9.0
Phillips H & N Cdn	R	05/71	Peter Guernsey (Incep)	23.3	17.63	+16.9	+15.4	+13.6	−6.8	−11.3	avg	avg	+0.27	−0.07	1.18	(b)
Dynamic American		08/79	S. Schulich	75.3	7.37	n.a.	+15.4	+12.6	−2.4	−14.7	avg −	avg	+0.28	−0.02	2.00	9.0
Templeton Growth		11/54	Templeton Invest. Coun.	1,284.7	17.11	+17.3	+15.3	+13.0	−9.5	−19.7	avg	avg	+0.28	−0.10	0.73	8.5
Industrial Equity	R	01/69	Mackenzie Invest. Mgrs.	178.2	20.56	+16.5	+15.0	+15.7	+0.4	−8.3	avg	avg	+0.28	−0.00	n.a.	9.0
B Tremblay Int'l		03/61	P. Spark	444.2	6.74	+19.6	+15.0	+14.0	−10.1	−20.5	avg +	avg	+0.19	−0.11	1.84	9.0
Cundill Value		12/67	Peter Cundill (13 yrs)	265.3	11.91	+21.2	+14.9	+14.7	+13.5	−3.2	avg −	avg	+0.41	+0.21	1.82	8.75
D K Enterprise	R	07/70	Dixon Krogseth Ltd(18yrs)	5.3	11.71	+16.8	+14.9	+27.1	+27.4	+20.8	avg +	avg +	+0.18	+0.19	2.41	1.0
Mackenzie Mortgage	R	12/74	Mackenzie Invest. Mgrs.	127.1	1.16	+13.1	+14.9	+16.2	+10.1	+5.8	avg	avg	+0.71	+0.48	n.a.	9.0

† Excludes Life Insurance (segregated) Funds

March 31, 1988
Mutual Funds Performance (All Categories)
10 years †

Fund name	RRSP & RRIF eligible	Launch date	Fund manager (Years)	Total net assets $ millions	Net asset value per share Mar.31, 1988	Average annual compound rate of return ‡ 10 yr. %	5 yr. %	3 yr. %	Simple rates of return 1 yr. %	6 mo. %	Variability 5 yr.	1 yr.	Reward/risk ratio 5 yr.	1 yr.	Expense ratio %	Maximum sales redempt. charge %
Mutual Funds; All Categories																
AGF Japan		01/69	R.J. Whiting	105.3	6.55	+23.5	+35.2	+42.5	+28.9	+2.3	avg +	avg +	+0.52	+0.30	1.56	9.0
MD Growth Investments		07/69	MD Management Ltd.	754.3	16.35	+22.5	+19.6	+18.9	−4.7	−17.7	avg	avg +	+0.31	−0.04	0.80	(q)
Formula Growth		06/60	J.W. Dobson (Incep)	n.a.	536.90	+22.1	+7.8	+8.3	−20.1	−24.1	avg +	avg +	+0.08	−0.15	1.48	(e)
AGF Special		09/68	R.J. Whiting	187.2	4.63	+21.8	+10.8	+10.4	−8.3	−15.9	avg	avg	+0.17	−0.09	1.48	9.0
Investors Japanese		03/71	I.G. Invest. Mgmt. Ltd.	194.6	16.47	+21.6	+32.2	+41.1	+32.3	+10.4	avg	avg −	+0.49	+0.50	1.32	8.5
Cundill Value		12/67	Peter Cundill (13 yrs)	265.3	11.91	+21.2	+14.9	+14.7	+13.5	−3.2	avg −	avg	+0.41	+0.21	1.82	8.75
B Tremblay Int'l		03/61	P. Spark	444.2	6.74	+19.6	+15.0	+14.0	−10.1	−20.5	avg +	avg	+0.19	−0.11	1.84	9.0
Mackenzie Equity	R	05/73	Mackenzie Invest. Mgrs.	70.0	2.42	+19.5	+15.7	+16.7	−1.7	−8.7	avg	avg	+0.28	−0.01	n.a.	9.0
Cdn Anaesthetists	R	11/57	Sceptre Invest. Counsel	56.4	9.70	+19.1	+13.4	+12.1	−8.8	−10.0	avg	avg	+0.26	−0.11	0.79	nil
Industrial American		07/75	Mackenzie Invest. Mgrs.	424.6	7.30	+19.0	+13.2	+12.0	−6.6	−16.4	avg	avg	+0.21	−0.06	n.a.	9.0
United Accum Retire	R	08/71	Gerald Coleman (9 yrs)	165.3	10.96	+19.0	+13.9	+10.0	−5.0	−4.6	avg −	avg	+0.35	−0.08	1.80	9.0
United Venture Retire	R	08/71	Gerald Coleman (9 yrs)	80.0	11.44	+19.0	+12.9	+10.8	−14.1	−13.0	avg	avg	+0.25	−0.17	1.83	9.0
Tradex	R	01/60	Sceptre Inv. Coun.	44.8	7.20	+18.7	+13.8	+11.7	−8.3	−10.1	avg	avg	+0.27	−0.11	1.13	nil
United Accumulative		05/57	Gerald Coleman (9 yrs)	241.3	9.82	+18.7	+14.1	+9.0	−13.2	−17.9	avg	avg	+0.27	−0.15	1.70	9.0
Cdn Security Growth	R	06/63	W. R. Farquharson	586.6	8.91	+18.6	+14.7	+11.4	−11.2	−12.1	avg	avg	+0.29	−0.14	1.68	9.0
Guardian Enterprise	R	11/72	Jim Cole (15 yrs)	51.6	1.04	+18.4	+13.4	+11.1	−5.6	−8.6	avg	avg	+0.22	−0.05	1.05	9.0
Royfund Equity	R	12/66	Martin Siegerman (15 yrs)	852.8	20.18	+18.4	+15.7	+13.6	−10.5	−13.4	avg	avg	+0.30	−0.13	0.51	nil
Goldfund		03/67	CSA Mgmt. Ltd.	13.7	5.98	+18.3	+6.3	+13.4	−16.0	−25.8	avg +	avg +	+0.06	−0.13	2.25	9.0
American Growth		04/57	W.D. Cameron	107.5	7.30	+18.1	+11.0	+8.2	−7.9	−16.0	avg	avg	+0.17	−0.08	1.48	9.0
Universal Savings Eq	R	04/65	Mackenzie Finl. (13 yrs)	118.3	10.95	+18.0	+16.4	+17.8	+3.6	−2.4	avg	avg	+0.32	+0.04	2.00	9.0
CMA Investment	R	03/66	MD Management Ltd.	863.3	28.62	+17.8	+16.3	+16.3	+3.0	−3.6	avg −	avg	+0.39	+0.04	0.75	(q)
Industrial Growth	R	10/67	Mackenzie Invest. Mgrs.	1,615.3	14.64	+17.8	+15.6	+16.0	+1.5	−6.7	avg	avg	+0.32	+0.01	n.a.	9.0
Confed Dolphin	R	10/72	Confed Invest. Mgmt. Ltd.	6.1	7.80	+17.6	+14.2	+12.6	−6.5	−9.3	avg	avg	+0.29	−0.08	1.50	5.5
Jones Heward	R	07/69	Gary Canlett	60.0	7.99	+17.5	+12.9	+12.3	−10.2	−11.2	avg	avg	+0.21	−0.10	1.80	9.0
Templeton Growth		11/54	Templeton Invest. Coun.	1,284.7	17.11	+17.3	+15.3	+13.0	−9.5	−19.7	avg	avg	+0.28	−0.10	0.73	8.5

† Excludes Life Insurance (Segregated) funds

Top 25 RRSP-eligible funds at March 31, 1988

5 year Returns – Canadian Equity Funds
March 31, 1983 – March 31, 1988

Fund name	RRSP & RRIF eligible	Launch date	Fund manager (Years)	Total net assets $ millions	Net asset value per share Mar.31, 1988	Average annual compound rate of return ‡ 10 yr. %	5 yr. %	3 yr. %	Simple rates of return 1 yr. %	6 mo. %	Variability 5 yr.	1 yr.	Reward/risk ratio 5 yr.	1 yr.	Expense ratio %	Maximum sales redempt. charge %
CANADIAN EQUITY FUNDS																
Trans-Canada Equity	R	01/72	Sagit Management	4.6	7.30	+16.5	+23.5	+24.5	−0.2	−1.1	avg	avg	+0.48	−0.00	2.00	8.75
Cambridge Growth	R	08/66	Sagit Management Ltd.	1.4	6.66	+16.6	+21.9	+22.6	−0.8	−3.5	avg	avg	+0.44	−0.01	2.00	8.75
Industrial Dividend	R	12/77	Mackenzie Invest. Mgrs.	269.4	10.82	+16.8	+17.5	+16.9	−0.7	−9.3	avg	avg	+0.31	−0.00	n.a.	9.0
Trans-Cda Shares C	R	12/50	Sagit Management	6.8	12.83	+14.3	+16.6	+18.9	+1.3	+2.4	avg −	avg −	+0.39	+0.02	1.92	(e)
Universal Savings Eq	R	04/65	Mackenzie Finl. (13 yrs)	118.3	10.95	+18.0	+16.4	+17.8	+3.6	−2.4	avg	avg	+0.32	+0.04	2.00	9.0
CMA Investment	R	03/66	MD Management Ltd.	863.3	28.62	+17.8	+16.3	+16.3	+3.0	−3.6	avg −	avg	+0.39	+0.04	0.75	(q)
Industrial Pension	R	02/71	Mackenzie Invest. Mgrs.	142.9	5.99	+16.0	+15.8	+16.1	−3.0	−10.0	avg	avg	+0.27	−0.03	n.a.	9.0
Royfund Equity	R	12/66	Martin Siegerman (15 yrs)	852.8	20.18	+18.4	+15.7	+13.6	−10.5	−13.4	avg	avg	+0.30	−0.13	0.51	nil
Mackenzie Equity	R	05/73	Mackenzie Invest. Mgrs.	70.0	2.42	+19.5	+15.7	+16.7	−1.7	−8.7	avg	avg	+0.28	−0.01	n.a.	9.0
Industrial Growth	R	10/67	Mackenzie Invest. Mgrs.	1,615.3	14.64	+17.8	+15.6	+16.0	+1.5	−6.7	avg	avg	+0.32	+0.01	n.a.	9.0
Phillips H & N Cdn	R	05/71	Peter Guernsey (Incep)	23.3	17.63	+16.9	+15.4	+13.6	−6.8	−11.3	avg	avg	+0.27	−0.07	1.18	(b)
Industrial Equity	R	01/69	Mackenzie Invest. Mgrs.	178.2	20.56	+16.5	+15.0	+15.7	+0.4	−8.3	avg	avg	+0.28	−0.00	n.a.	9.0
CDA Common Stock	R	05/58	Impco Invest. Mgmt(4 yrs)	33.1	13.26	+16.2	+14.7	+13.9	−9.7	−13.2	avg	avg	+0.28	−0.12	n.a.	nil
Cdn Security Growth	R	06/63	W. R. Farquharson	586.6	8.91	+18.6	+14.7	+11.4	−11.2	−12.1	avg	avg	+0.29	−0.14	1.68	9.0
Trimark Canadian	R	09/81	Trimark Invest. Mgmt.	444.1	10.25	n.a.	+14.7	+12.4	−2.2	−10.2	avg	avg	+0.28	−0.02	1.62	9.0
NW Canadian	R	07/65	Phillips Hager & North	6.0	7.70	+15.7	+14.6	+13.8	−10.2	−13.8	avg	avg	+0.25	−0.10	2.00	(j)
Confed Dolphin	R	10/72	Confed Invest. Mgmt. Ltd.	6.1	7.80	+17.6	+14.2	+12.6	−6.5	−9.3	avg	avg	+0.29	−0.08	1.50	5.5
Phillips H & N Retiremt	R	12/71	Peter Guernsey (Incep)	14.3	51.54	+14.7	+14.0	+12.1	−9.8	−14.7	avg	avg	+0.23	−0.09	1.26	2.0
United Accum Retire	R	08/71	Gerald Coleman (9 yrs)	165.3	10.96	+19.0	+13.9	+10.0	−5.0	−4.6	avg −	avg	+0.35	−0.08	1.80	9.0
Tradex	R	01/60	Sceptre Inv. Coun.	44.8	7.20	+18.7	+13.8	+11.7	−8.3	−10.1	avg	avg	+0.27	−0.11	1.13	nil
Cundill Security	R	79	Peter Cundill (13 yrs)	18.7	14.11	n.a.	+13.8	+12.9	+0.6	−4.8	avg −	avg −	+0.35	+0.01	1.58	8.75
Guardian Enterprise	R	11/72	Jim Cole (15 yrs)	51.6	1.04	+18.4	+13.4	+11.1	−5.6	−8.6	avg	avg	+0.22	−0.05	1.05	9.0
Cdn Anaesthetists	R	11/57	Sceptre Invest. Counsel	56.4	9.70	+19.1	+13.4	+12.1	−8.8	−10.0	avg	avg	+0.26	−0.11	0.79	nil
Talvest Growth	R	07/47	T.A.L. Invest. Counsel	61.7	8.94	+14.9	+13.0	+13.6	−4.0	−7.5	avg	avg	+0.26	−0.05	1.74	9.0
United Venture Retire	R	08/71	Gerald Coleman (9 yrs)	80.0	11.44	+19.0	+12.9	+10.8	−14.1	−13.0	avg	avg	+0.25	−0.17	1.83	9.0

Top 25 RRSP-eligible funds at March 31, 1988

10 year Returns — Canadian Equity Funds
March 31, 1978 — March 31, 1988

Fund name	RRSP & RRIF eligible	Launch date	Fund manager (Years)	Total net assets $ millions Mar.31, 1988	Net asset value per share Mar.31, 1988	Average annual compound rate of return ‡ 10 yr. %	Average annual compound rate of return 5 yr. %	Average annual compound rate of return 3 yr. %	Simple rates of return 1 yr. %	Simple rates of return 6 mo. %	Variability 5 yr.	Variability 1 yr.	Reward/risk ratio 5 yr.	Reward/risk ratio 1 yr.	Expense ratio %	Maximum sales redempt. charge %
CANADIAN EQUITY FUNDS																
Mackenzie Equity	R	05/73	Mackenzie Invest. Mgrs.	70.0	2.42	+19.5	+15.7	+16.7	−1.7	−8.7	avg	avg	+0.28	−0.01	n.a.	9.0
Cdn Anaesthetists	R	11/57	Sceptre Invest. Counsel	56.4	9.70	+19.1	+13.4	+12.1	−8.8	−10.0	avg	avg	+0.26	−0.11	0.79	nil
United Venture Retire	R	08/71	Gerald Coleman (9 yrs)	80.0	11.44	+19.0	+12.9	+10.8	−14.1	−13.0	avg	avg	+0.25	−0.17	1.83	9.0
United Accum Retire	R	08/71	Gerald Coleman (9 yrs)	165.3	10.96	+19.0	+13.9	+10.0	−5.0	−4.6	avg –	avg	+0.35	−0.08	1.80	9.0
Tradex	R	01/60	Sceptre Inv. Coun.	44.8	7.20	+18.7	+13.8	+11.7	−8.3	−10.1	avg	avg	+0.27	−0.11	1.13	nil
Cdn Security Growth	R	06/63	W. R. Farquharson	586.6	8.91	+18.6	+14.7	+11.4	−11.2	−12.1	avg	avg	+0.29	−0.14	1.68	9.0
Guardian Enterprise	R	11/72	Jim Cole (15 yrs)	51.6	1.04	+18.4	+13.4	+11.1	−5.6	−8.6	avg	avg	+0.22	−0.05	1.05	9.0
Royfund Equity	R	12/66	Martin Siegerman (15 yrs)	852.8	20.18	+18.4	+15.7	+13.6	−10.5	−13.4	avg	avg	+0.30	−0.13	0.51	nil
Universal Savings Eq	R	04/65	Mackenzie Finl. (13 yrs)	118.3	10.95	+18.0	+16.4	+17.8	+3.6	−2.4	avg	avg	+0.32	+0.04	2.00	9.0
Industrial Growth	R	10/67	Mackenzie Invest. Mgrs.	1,615.3	14.64	+17.8	+15.6	+16.0	+1.5	−6.7	avg	avg	+0.32	+0.01	n.a.	9.0
CMA Investment	R	03/66	MD Management Ltd.	863.3	28.62	+17.8	+16.3	+16.3	+3.0	−3.6	avg –	avg	+0.39	+0.04	0.75	(q)
Confed Dolphin	R	10/72	Confed Invest. Mgmt. Ltd.	6.1	7.80	+17.6	+14.2	+12.6	−6.5	−9.3	avg	avg	+0.29	−0.08	1.50	5.5
Jones Heward	R	07/69	Gary Canlett	60.0	7.99	+17.5	+12.9	+12.3	−10.2	−11.2	avg	avg	+0.21	−0.10	1.80	9.0
Growth Equity	R	10/64	W. R. Farquharson	154.4	9.60	+17.1	+11.1	+11.1	−21.5	−21.6	avg	avg	+0.16	−0.20	1.63	9.0
Phillips H & N Cdn	R	05/71	Peter Guernsey (Incep)	23.3	17.63	+16.9	+15.4	+13.6	−6.8	−11.3	avg	avg	+0.27	−0.07	1.18	(b)
Industrial Dividend	R	12/77	Mackenzie Invest. Mgrs.	269.4	10.82	+16.8	+17.5	+16.9	−0.7	−9.3	avg	avg	+0.31	−0.00	n.a.	9.0
Cambridge Growth	R	08/66	Sagit Management Ltd.	1.4	6.66	+16.6	+21.9	+22.6	−0.8	−3.5	avg	avg	+0.44	−0.01	2.00	8.75
Industrial Equity	R	01/69	Mackenzie Invest. Mgrs.	178.2	20.56	+16.5	+15.0	+15.7	+0.4	−8.3	avg	avg	+0.28	−0.00	n.a.	9.0
Trans-Canada Equity	R	01/72	Sagit Management	4.6	7.30	+16.5	+23.5	+24.5	−0.2	−1.1	avg	avg	+0.48	−0.00	2.00	8.75
Guaranty Tr Mgd Equ R ..	R	05/65	Guaranty Trust Co.	149.9	4.33	+16.3	+11.8	+8.6	−12.0	−14.1	avg	avg	+0.23	−0.13	2.00	nil
Dynamic Canada	R	07/57	S. Schulich (12 yrs)	189.5	12.64	+16.3	+11.1	+14.5	−1.8	−7.6	avg	avg	+0.24	−0.02	2.00	9.0
CDA Common Stock	R	05/58	Impco Invest. Mgmt(4 yrs)	33.1	13.26	+16.2	+14.7	+13.9	−9.7	−13.2	avg	avg	+0.28	−0.12	n.a.	nil
Guaranty Tr Inv Equ R ...	R	01/62	Guaranty Trust Co.	30.1	5.82	+16.0	+11.4	+9.2	−12.4	−15.2	avg	avg	+0.22	−0.13	2.13	nil
Industrial Pension	R	02/71	Mackenzie Invest. Mgrs.	142.9	5.99	+16.0	+15.8	+16.1	−3.0	−10.0	avg	avg	+0.27	−0.03	n.a.	9.0
NW Canadian	R	07/65	Phillips Hager & North	6.0	7.70	+15.7	+14.6	+13.8	−10.2	−13.8	avg	avg	+0.25	−0.10	2.00	(j)

Top 25 RRSP-eligible fixed income funds at March 31, 1988

5 year Returns — Fixed Income Funds
March 31, 1983 — March 31, 1988

Fund name	RRSP & RRIF eligible	Launch date	Fund manager (Years)	Total net assets $ millions Mar.31, 1988	Net asset value per share Mar.31, 1988	Average annual compound rate of return ‡ 10 yr. %	Average annual compound rate of return 5 yr. %	Average annual compound rate of return 3 yr. %	Simple rates of return 1 yr. %	Simple rates of return 6 mo. %	Variability 5 yr.	Variability 1 yr.	Reward/risk ratio 5 yr.	Reward/risk ratio 1 yr.	Expense ratio %	Maximum sales redempt. charge %
FIXED INCOME FUNDS																
Industrial Income	R	07/74	Mackenzie Invest. Mgrs.	117.0	10.00	+11.5	+15.8	+17.4	+11.2	+6.5	avg	avg	+0.68	+0.61	n.a.	9.0
Mackenzie Mortgage	R	12/74	Mackenzie Invest. Mgrs.	127.1	1.16	+13.1	+14.9	+16.2	+10.1	+5.8	avg	avg	+0.71	+0.48	n.a.	9.0
Phillips H & N Bond	R	11/70	A.R. Gage (4 yrs)	44.7	8.78	+11.5	+13.9	+15.9	+9.0	+13.7	avg	avg	+0.50	+0.32	0.68	(b)
Canadian Trusteed	R	08/62	C.W. Goldring	351.5	4.67	+11.6	+13.5	+13.5	+2.4	+14.0	avg +	avg +	+0.45	+0.05	0.76	9.0
Universal Savings Inc	R	08/75	Mackenzie Financial	12.7	5.26	+10.5	+13.2	+14.9	+9.5	+10.2	avg +	avg	+0.45	+0.34	1.46	9.0
Talvest Bond	R	04/72	T.A.L. Invest. Counsel	10.8	10.25	+11.9	+13.2	+13.5	+5.3	+11.7	avg	avg	+0.50	+0.14	1.58	9.0
Canada Trust RSP Income	R	10/57	C.T. Invest. Coun.(Incep)	170.7	43.50	+11.2	+13.0	+12.6	+5.1	+10.2	avg	avg	+0.60	+0.17	0.71	nil
Genl Tr Bond	R	11/66	Investment Dept.	79.1	9.62	+11.3	+12.9	+13.6	+3.3	+10.3	avg	avg	+0.46	+0.09	1.01	nil
Mtl Trust RSP Inc Sec	R	02/58	Montrusco Associates Inc.	79.9	18.09	+10.9	+12.2	+13.4	+3.0	+9.2	avg	avg	+0.59	+0.12	n.a.	nil
General Trust Mortgage	R	06/72	Investment Dept.	47.4	10.70	+11.4	+12.1	+11.5	+6.8	+6.3	avg −	avg −	+1.16	+0.69	1.22	nil
Fonds des Prof. Bonds	R	03/78	Fonds des Prof. du Quebec	n.a.	105.13	+12.2	+12.0	+12.4	+5.3	+8.4	avg	avg	+0.76	+0.29	0.75	nil
Mtl Trust RSP Mtge Sec	R	02/74	Montreal Trust	61.6 (d)	10.11	+11.5	+12.0	+12.7	+15.5	+13.5	avg −	avg	+0.96	+0.63	n.a.	nil
Montreal Trust Income	R	12/64	Montrusco Associates Inc.	18.4	8.41	+10.3	+12.0	+13.9	+2.6	+7.6	avg	avg	+0.52	+0.09	1.09	nil
Royal Trust Bond	R	12/67	Corp. Invest. Assoc.	308.6	9.07	+10.9	+12.0	+12.3	+2.9	+11.4	avg +	avg	+0.41	+0.08	1.12	nil
Viking Income	R	11/72	Multiple	115.7	4.10	+9.7	+11.9	+12.2	+2.1	+11.3	avg	avg	+0.45	+0.05	1.03	(f)
Dynamic Income	R	08/79	Beutel Goodman (Incep)	89.2	5.32	n.a.	+11.8	+11.0	+6.1	+4.6	avg	avg	+0.63	+0.44	1.00	5.0
National Trust Income	R	09/57	National Trust	11.8	77.50	+10.5	+11.7	+12.4	+5.7	+8.3	avg	avg	+0.44	+0.23	n.a.	nil
Prudential Income	R	01/75	Prudential Fund Mgt.	41.4	5.18	+10.7	+11.6	+11.5	+6.0	+8.9	avg	avg	+0.79	+0.30	1.00	8.5
First Canadian Mortgage	R	07/74	Board of Trustees(13 yrs)	500.5	11.34	+14.5	+11.6	+11.5	+8.2	+7.2	avg −	avg −	+1.24	+0.88	1.08	(u)
CDA Fixed Income	R	05/70	Impco Invest. Mgmt(4 yrs)	20.6	60.85	+11.4	+11.6	+12.2	+4.8	+9.9	avg	avg	+0.60	+0.15	n.a.	nil
Investors Bond	R	04/79	I.G. Invest. Mgmt. Ltd.	551.3	4.28	n.a.	+11.6	+12.4	+3.2	+12.1	avg	avg	+0.44	+0.08	1.32	8.5
Royal Trust Mortgage	R	12/68	Corp. Invest. Assoc.	1,029.8	10.57	+11.6	+11.4	+11.3	+8.0	+7.4	avg	avg −	+0.77	+0.77	1.36	nil
Dolphin Mortgage	R	01/76	Confed Invest. Mgmt. Ltd.	3.3	5.13	+11.9	+11.3	+11.2	+8.6	+6.5	avg −	avg −	+1.37	+1.25	1.50	2.5
Investors Mortgage	R	10/73	I.G. Invest. Mgmt. Ltd.	1,123.4	5.00	+11.2	+11.2	+10.8	+7.1	+6.9	avg	avg −	+0.79	+0.71	1.30	8.5
Fonds Desjard Hypo	R	08/65		100.8	4.43	+11.4	+11.1	+11.2	+8.9	+6.8	avg	avg −	+0.70	+1.35	n.a.	nil

Top 25 RRSP-eligible fixed income funds at March 31, 1988

10 year Returns – Fixed Income Funds
March 31, 1978 – March 31, 1988

Fund name	RRSP & RRIF eligible	Launch date	Fund manager (Years)	Total net assets $ millions Mar.31, 1988	Net asset value per share Mar.31, 1988	Average annual compound rate of return ‡ 10 yr. %	5 yr. %	3 yr. %	Simple rates of return 1 yr. %	6 mo. %	Variability 5 yr.	1 yr.	Reward/risk ratio 5 yr.	1 yr.	Expense ratio %	Maximum sales redempt. charge %
FIXED INCOME FUNDS																
First Canadian Mortgage	R	07/74	Board of Trustees(13 yrs)	500.5	11.34	+14.5	+11.6	+11.5	+8.2	+7.2	avg –	avg –	+1.24	+0.88	1.08	(u)
Mackenzie Mortgage	R	12/74	Mackenzie Invest. Mgrs.	127.1	1.16	+13.1	+14.9	+16.2	+10.1	+5.8	avg	avg	+0.71	+0.48	n.a.	9.0
Fonds des Prof. Bonds	R	03/78	Fonds des Prof. du Quebec	n.a.	105.13	+12.2	+12.0	+12.4	+5.3	+8.4	avg	avg	+0.76	+0.29	0.75	nil
Dolphin Mortgage	R	01/76	Confed Invest. Mgmt. Ltd.	3.3	5.13	+11.9	+11.3	+11.2	+8.6	+6.5	avg –	avg –	+1.37	+1.25	1.50	2.5
Talvest Bond	R	04/72	T.A.L. Invest. Counsel	10.8	10.25	+11.9	+13.2	+13.5	+5.3	+11.7	avg	avg	+0.50	+0.14	1.58	9.0
All-Cdn Revenue	R	09/68	Philip Spicer	1.8	3.41	+11.9	+9.9	+9.9	+7.6	+5.4	avg	avg –	+0.71	+1.13	1.89	9.0
Altamira	R	05/70	Multiple (Incep)	6.3	6.31	+11.8	+11.0	+10.9	+7.8	+9.9	avg	avg	+0.64	+0.34	1.00	nil
Canadian Trusteed	R	08/62	C.W. Goldring	351.5	4.67	+11.6	+13.5	+13.5	+2.4	+14.0	avg +	avg +	+0.45	+0.05	0.76	9.0
Royal Trust Mortgage	R	12/68	Corp. Invest. Assoc.	1,029.8	10.57	+11.6	+11.4	+11.3	+8.0	+7.4	avg	avg –	+0.77	+0.77	1.36	nil
Phillips H & N Bond	R	11/70	A.R. Gage (4 yrs)	44.7	8.78	+11.5	+13.9	+15.9	+9.0	+13.7	avg	avg	+0.50	+0.32	0.68	(b)
Mtl Trust RSP Mtge Sec	R	02/74	Montreal Trust	61.6 (d)	10.11	+11.5	+12.0	+12.7	+15.5	+13.5	avg –	avg	+0.96	+0.63	n.a.	nil
Industrial Income	R	07/74	Mackenzie Invest. Mgrs.	117.0	10.00	+11.5	+15.8	+17.4	+11.2	+6.5	avg	avg	+0.68	+0.61	n.a.	9.0
Fonds Desjard Hypo	R	08/65		100.8	4.43	+11.4	+11.1	+11.2	+8.9	+6.8	avg	avg –	+0.70	+1.35	n.a.	nil
General Trust Mortgage	R	06/72	Investment Dept.	47.4	10.70	+11.4	+12.1	+11.5	+6.8	+6.3	avg –	avg –	+1.16	+0.69	1.22	nil
CDA Fixed Income	R	05/70	Impco Invest. Mgmt(4 yrs)	20.6	60.85	+11.4	+11.6	+12.2	+4.8	+9.9	avg	avg	+0.60	+0.15	n.a.	nil
Canada Trust Mortgage	R	01/75	C.T. Invest. Coun.(Incep)	126.3	38.48	+11.3	+11.1	+11.1	+8.9	+6.8	avg –	avg	+1.10	+0.65	1.06	nil
Genl Tr Bond	R	11/66	Investment Dept.	79.1	9.62	+11.3	+12.9	+13.6	+3.3	+10.3	avg	avg	+0.46	+0.09	1.01	nil
Investors Mortgage	R	10/73	I.G. Invest. Mgmt. Ltd.	1,123.4	5.00	+11.2	+11.2	+10.8	+7.1	+6.9	avg	avg –	+0.79	+0.71	1.30	8.5
Canada Trust RSP Income	R	10/57	C.T. Invest. Coun.(Incep)	170.7	43.50	+11.2	+13.0	+12.6	+5.1	+10.2	avg	avg	+0.60	+0.17	0.71	nil
TD's Green Line Mtge	R	12/73	Board of Trustees	63.4	10.53	+11.1	+10.1	+9.8	+9.2	+7.5	avg	avg	+0.64	+0.55	1.15	nil
Montreal Trust Mortgage	R	12/74	Montreal Trust Co.	18.8	10.09	+11.0	+10.8	+10.4	+7.7	+6.2	avg	avg +	+0.47	+0.15	1.59	nil
Mtl Trust RSP Inc Sec	R	02/58	Montrusco Associates Inc.	79.9	18.09	+10.9	+12.2	+13.4	+3.0	+9.2	avg	avg	+0.59	+0.12	n.a.	nil
Royal Trust Bond	R	12/67	Corp. Invest. Assoc.	308.6	9.07	+10.9	+12.0	+12.3	+2.9	+11.4	avg +	avg	+0.41	+0.08	1.12	nil
CIBC Mortgage Investment	R	12/74	CIBC Invest. Mgmt.	46.6	11.08	+10.9	+10.7	+10.8	+8.8	+6.9	avg	avg	+0.72	+0.64	1.17	nil
Prudential Income	R	01/75	Prudential Fund Mgt.	41.4	5.18	+10.7	+11.6	+11.5	+6.0	+8.9	avg	avg	+0.79	+0.30	1.00	8.5

March 31, 1988
Mutual Funds Performance (All Categories)
Insurance Funds — 5 years

Fund name	RRSP & RRIF eligible	Launch date	Fund manager (Years)	Total net assets $ millions Mar.31, 1988	Net asset value per share Mar.31, 1988	Average annual compound rate of return ‡ 10 yr. %	5 yr. %	3 yr. %	Simple rates of return 1 yr. %	6 mo. %	Variability 5 yr.	Variability 1 yr.	Reward/risk ratio 5 yr.	Reward/risk ratio 1 yr.	Expense ratio %	Maximum sales redempt. charge %
Mutual Funds - All Categories (Insurance)																
Impco Ret Growth		03/69	Imperial Life	n.a.	97.50	+19.8	+19.3	+22.6	+5.8	−7.0	avg +	avg +	+0.30	+0.05	n.a.	
Confed Life C	R	12/70	Confederation Life	n.a.	6.98	+13.9	+17.7	+15.2	+7.5	+14.0	avg +	avg +	+0.57	+0.13	1.44	
Canada Life E.2	R	11/62	Can. Life Inv Mgt (3 yrs)	7.7	153.44	+17.4	+15.3	+13.8	−7.5	−10.9	avg	avg	+0.26	−0.08	1.00	
Crown Life (CCIFA)	R	07/68	Beutel, Goodman & Co. Ltd.	33.4	56.38	+13.6	+14.9	+18.1	−5.9	−11.0	avg	avg	+0.26	−0.06	n.a.	
Empire Life Fund 3	R	01/71	Donald Miano (2 years)	33.5	11.47	+21.3	+14.9	+16.9	−5.8	−5.6	avg	avg −	+0.26	−0.07	1.20	
Canada Life S.9	R	08/69	Can. Life Inv Mgt (3 yrs)	171.5	70.65	+16.5	+14.2	+12.7	−6.2	−8.1	avg	avg −	+0.27	−0.07	2.00	
Confed Life A		01/69	Confederation Life	n.a.	12.05	+16.3	+14.2	+11.2	−6.7	−7.1	avg −	avg	+0.28	−0.08	0.48	
London Life Bond	R	12/61	Charles Hughson (4 yrs)	217.1	78.22	+12.1	+14.2	+14.3	−2.9	+9.0	avg +	avg +	+0.38	−0.05	0.98	
Cdn General Life A	R	06/68	Guaranty Tr. Co.	3.4	117.45	+17.8	+14.1	+11.4	−9.7	−13.0	avg	avg	+0.23	−0.10	1.38	
Confed Life B	R	01/69	Confederation Life	n.a.	11.36	+16.1	+14.1	+11.7	−4.2	−6.4	avg −	avg −	+0.28	−0.05	0.96	
Nat'l Life Fixed	R	12/62	Nang Cheung (3 yrs)	3.0	77.82	+12.4	+14.0	+14.0	+5.0	+11.0	avg	avg	+0.58	+0.16	n.a.	
Nat'l Life Equities	R	05/61	Jim Blake (9 yrs.)	18.7	156.47	+16.7	+13.9	+12.5	−4.8	−11.8	avg	avg	+0.24	−0.55	n.a.	
Nat'l Life of Cda	R	10/71	Jim Blake (9 yrs.)	0.7	62.74	+16.2	+13.9	+11.8	−7.5	−13.3	avg	avg	+0.24	−0.08	n.a.	
L'Assur-Vie Desjard Bond		01/66		14.7	62.49	+11.6	+13.8	+13.4	+3.4	+11.4	avg	avg	+0.56	+0.09	n.a.	
Empire Life Fund 5	R	12/69	Donald Miano (12 yrs)	2.0	55.28	+20.5	+13.7	+11.1	−16.9	−19.9	avg +	avg +	+0.21	−0.16	0.50	

March 31, 1988
Mutual Funds Performance (All Categories)
Insurance Funds — 10 years

Fund name	RRSP & RRIF eligible	Launch date	Fund manager (Years)	Total net assets $ millions Mar.31, 1988	Net asset value per share Mar.31, 1988	Average annual compound rate of return ‡ 10 yr. %	5 yr. %	3 yr. %	Simple rates of return 1 yr. %	6 mo. %	Variability 5 yr.	1 yr.	Reward/risk ratio 5 yr.	1 yr.	Expense ratio %	Maximum sales redempt. charge %
Mutual Funds - All Categories (Insurance)																
Empire Life Fund 3	R	01/71	Donald Miano (2 years)	33.5	11.47	+21.3	+14.9	+16.9	−5.8	−5.6	avg	avg −	+0.26	−0.07	1.20	
Empire Life Fund 5	R	12/69	Donald Miano (12 yrs)	2.0	55.28	+20.5	+13.7	+11.1	−16.9	−19.9	avg +	avg +	+0.21	−0.16	0.50	
Impco Ret Growth		03/69	Imperial Life	n.a.	97.50	+19.8	+19.3	+22.6	+5.8	−7.0	avg +	avg +	+0.30	+0.05	n.a.	
Empire Life Fund 1	R	64	Donald Miano (12 yrs.)	133.9	43.03	+19.2	+13.0	+14.3	−3.2	−8.3	avg	avg	+0.23	−0.03	1.20	
Cdn General Life A	R	06/68	Guaranty Tr. Co.	3.4	117.45	+17.8	+14.1	+11.4	−9.7	−13.0	avg	avg	+0.23	−0.10	1.38	
Mutual Life B	R	11/71	Mucana Investment (Incep)	12.9	67.82	+17.8	+12.9	+9.8	−9.6	−11.0	avg	avg +	+0.21	−0.09	n.a.	
Canada Life E.2	R	11/62	Can. Life Inv Mgt (3 yrs)	7.7	153.44	+17.4	+15.3	+13.8	−7.5	−10.9	avg	avg	+0.26	−0.08	1.00	
L'Assur-Vie Desjard Stock		01/66		13.4	78.85	+17.3	+12.9	+13.4	−15.1	−17.5	avg	avg	+0.23	−0.17	n.a.	
London Life Equity	R	12/61	Rohit Sehgal (6 yrs)	142.3	120.01	+17.2	+13.4	+12.6	−7.0	−12.4	avg	avg	+0.24	−0.08	0.98	
Canadian Reassurance ..		06/69	M. Corbett (15 yrs)	0.8	75.47	+17.0	+13.4	+12.7	−11.7	−15.5	avg	avg	+0.23	−0.13	n.a.	
Nat'l Life Equities	R	05/61	Jim Blake (9 yrs.)	18.7	156.47	+16.7	+13.9	+12.5	−4.8	−11.8	avg	avg	+0.24	−0.55	n.a.	
Canada Life S.9	R	08/69	Can. Life Inv Mgt (3 yrs)	171.5	70.65	+16.5	+14.2	+12.7	−6.2	−8.1	avg	avg −	+0.27	−0.07	2.00	
MONY Canadian Growth .	R	07/74	Tor.Invest.Mgmt.(Incep)	123.9	55.11	+16.4	+9.8	+8.2	−21.6	−16.6	avg −	avg	+0.19	−0.26	2.00	
Confed Life A		01/69	Confederation Life	n.a.	12.05	+16.3	+14.2	+11.2	−6.7	−7.1	avg −	avg	+0.28	−0.08	0.48	
Citadel Life	R	07/70	Patty Stewart(1 yr)	5.1	8.78	+16.2	+10.4	+10.1	−10.2	−13.2	avg	avg +	+0.17	−0.09	0.77	

Index

A.H. Robins Company, 37
Administration costs, 65
Advertising of funds, 74
AGF Growth Equity Fund, 57
AGF Japan Fund, 15, 41
AGF Management Limited, 14-15, 29, 88, 114-115
AGF Special Fund, 15, 25
AIC Investment Planning Limited, 131
All-Canadian Venture Fund, 120
All-weather funds, 92-93
Allied Fund, 29
Altamira Management Limited, 16
Andrew, Elaine, 128-130
Annual compound rate of return, 84
Annuities, 73
Arbitrage, 47
Asbestos scandal, 37
Associate Investors Fund, 86
Average annual compound rate of return, 142
Averaging plan, 99

12b-1 plans, 67
Bache Group Incorporated, 120
Back-end load, 67
Balanced funds, 33, 93, 151, 156, 159, 160
Bank of Montreal, 43, 136
Bank of Nova Scotia, 136
Banks, and mutual funds, 135-136
Bell Canada Enterprises, 25
Blue-chip equity funds, 25-26
Bolton Tremblay Funds Incorporated, 29, 87, 110
Bolton Tremblay Incorporated, 136
Bolton Tremblay International Fund, 41, 85, 112, 113
Bond funds, 27, 31
"Bottom-up" approach, 23, 104, 107, 116
Boyda, Bob, 135
BPI Capital Corporation, 15
British Columbia Resources Corporation, 120

CAFP (Canadian Association of Financial Planners), 128
Calvin Bullock Limited, 5
Cameron, Bill, 15
Canada Cumulative Fund, 112, 113
Canada Permanent Trust Company, 110
Canadian Association of Financial Planners (CAFP), 29
Canadian Deposit Insurance Corporation (CDIC), 29
Canadian equity funds, 146-148, 156, 158, 160
Canadian Imperial Bank of Commerce, 135-136
Canadian Investment Fund, 5
Canadian Mutual Funds Association, 6, 9
Canadian Pacific Enterprises, 25
Canadian Securities Institute, 62
Canadian Security Growth Fund, 115
Capital gains, 37, 76-78
Capital-gains tax exemption, 10, 55
CDIC (Canadian Deposit Insurance Corporation), 29
Charges, for buying, 63
Charlton, Richard, 130
Christ, Alexander, 14, 26
Closed-end funds, 45-52
  discount, 46, 47
  history, 46-47
  premium, 46

Co-mingling fund assets, 75
Coleman, Gerald, 41
Commercial mortgages, 30
Commissions, 11, 12, 62, 86
(*See also* Sales fees)
Commodity funds, 137
Commodity futures contracts, 22
Condliffe, Toby, 124-128
Confederation Life Insurance, 135
Consumer attitudes survey, 133-134
Convertible shares, 32
Cornfeld, Bernie, 6-9
Crane, John, 137
CSA Management Limited, 103
Cumulative preferred shares, 32
Cundill, Peter, 26, 87, 117-121
Cundill Security Fund, 83, 93, 118
Cundill Value Fund, 26, 85, 87, 118, 119
Currency hedging funds, 137

Dalkon Shield, 37
De Thomas Financial Corporation, 56
De Thomasis, Tony, 56-59, 98
Decima Research Limited, 133-134
Desmarais, Paul, 12
Diversification, 3
Diversified guaranteed investment, 138
Dividend funds, 27, 32, 152, 156, 160
Dividend tax credit, 32, 55
Dividends, 78-79
  mutual fund corporation, 79-80
  mutual fund trust, 79-80
  tax implications, 76
Dollar-cost averaging, 94
Dollar-cost averaging plan, 69
  contractual, 69
  voluntary, 69
Dow Jones Industrial Average, 10
Dynamic American Fund, 93
Dynamic Funds Management Incorporated, 16, 93, 94
Dynamic Managed Portfolio, 58

Eaton Group, 41
Elliott and Page Limited, 97
Equity funds, 84
  Canadian, 42
  U.S., 42
  (*See also* Stock funds)
Ethical funds, 36-37, 137
Ethical Growth Fund, 36
Ethics, sales agents, 74
Europe, Australia and Far East Index, 43
Excelsior Life Insurance Company, 110
Exchange-rate, 36
Expense ratios, 65-66, 89, 143
Ezra, Don, 103-104

Farquharson, Robert, 15, 114-117
Fees, 138
  (*See also* Management fees, Sales fees)
Fidelity Management, 134
Financial goals, 82
Financial planners, 10, 124
Financial Post, 6
Financial Post Guide to Mutual Funds, 17
Financial Post Mutual fund performance survey, 146-169
First Canadian Equity Index Fund, 43
Fixed Dollar Withdrawal Plan, 73
Fixed income funds, 85 149-150, 156, 159, 160
Fixed Period Withdrawal Plan, 73
Fixed-income funds, 26-28
FoodFund, 39

Foreign & Colonial Government
Trust, 4
Foreign funds, 85
Foreign investments, 137
Foreign tax credit, 80
Front-end sales charges, 9
Fund of Funds, 7
Fund management, 93-94
Fund manager (years), 141
Fund options, 88
FutureFund Shares Incorporated,
39

General Electric Company, 110
Global funds, 40-41
Globe and Mail, 127
"Go-go" era, 104
"Go-go" funds, 5-6, 24
GoldenFund, 39
Goldman Sachs and Company, 127
Goldring, Warren, 15
Government Bond Index Fund, 43
Graham, Reverend Billy, 108
Great Pacific Management
Company, 61
Green Line Canadian Index Fund,
42
Green Line Investors Service, 64
Green Line U.S. Index Fund, 42
Greenshields Incorporated, 120
Growth Equity Fund, 115
Growth funds, 24-25
Guaranty Trust Company of
Canada, 87, 112, 114
Guardian Capital Group Limited,
16, 39
Guardian Capital Incorporated, 50

Herzfeld, Thomas, 47-52
Hume Group Limited, 15-16

IFIC (Investment Funds Institute
of Canada), 16, 27, 61, 62, 75, 133
Imperial Advisors Limited, 38
Imperial Realty Growth Fund, 38
Incentives, sales agents, 74
Index funds, 42-43
Industrial Equity Fund, 58
Industrial Growth Fund, 26
Industrial Horizon Fund, 67
Insurance industry, and mutual
funds, 135
Interest rates, 30, 31, 32
International Controls
Corporation, 8
International equity funds, 155,
160
International Fund, 113
International funds, 40
International money market
funds, 157
Investment Dealer's Association,
63
Investment Funds Institute of
Canada (IFIC), 16, 27, 61, 62, 75,
133
Investment plan, 91
Investment strategy, RRSP, 55
Investors Group, 11, 29, 88, 123,
134, 136
Investors Group Fund, 128
Investors Group Incorporated, 4,
5, 12-13, 38, 100
Investors Group Limited, 36
Investors Japan Fund, 41
Investors Overseas Services
Limited (IOS), 6-9
fraud charges, 8-9
Investors Real Property Fund, 38
IOS (Investors Overseas Services
Limited), 6-9
fraud charges, 8-9

J. Walter Thompson Company,
120
Japanese funds, 15, 21, 41, 84, 154
Japanese securities, 35

"Know your client" rule, 70
Krembil, Robert, 41, 87, 108-111

Launch date, 141
Leblanc, Norman, 8-9
Lett, Tristram, 103
Leverage, 95
Life insurance funds, 158-160
LifeFund, 39
Lifetime capital-gains exemption, 77
Liquidity, 88
Literature, sales, 75
Load fund, 70
Load (*See* Sales fees)
Loads, front-end, 9
London Life Bond Fund, 57

McCutcheon, Fred, 16
McEwen, Rob, 103
McKelvey, Kent, 56-59
MacKenzie Equity Fund, 58
MacKenzie Financial Corporation, 13-14, 26, 67, 100
MacKenzie Mortgage and Income Fund, 57
McLeod Young Weir, 121
Magna International Incorporated, 108
Management:
  changes, 88
  companies, 100
  fees, 63, 65-66, 86
Managers, 51, 86
  compensation of, 102
Manufacturers Life Insurance Company, 115
Manville Corporation, 37
Marathon Brown and Company, 64
Margin, buying stocks on, 22
Market benchmarks, 161
Market break, 1969, 24
Marketing, 10-11
Massachusetts Investors Trust, 5
Mauro, Arthur, 13
Maximum sales and redemption charge, 143
Moneyletter, The, 16
Money-market funds, 27, 28-29, 153, 157, 159, 160
Monthly rate of return, 83
Morgan Guaranty Trust Company, 120
Morgan Stanley Capital
  International, 43
  World Index, 40
Morrison, Russ, 110
Mortgage funds, 27, 30
Mortgages:
  commercial, 30
  residential, 30
Multiple Opportunities Fund, 24
Mutual fund(s):
  concept, 11
  corporations, 71, 76-77
  crash, 1969, 6
  definition, 2
  "family", 88
  future entrants, 134-139
  growth of, 2
  history, 4-5
  investor profile, 4
  performance, 92, 93, 162, 163, 168, 169
  pros and cons, 3-4
  restrictions, 73-74
  sales, 61
  salespeople, 123-132
  trusts, 76-77
Mutual Life Assurance Company of Canada, 135
Mutual-fund units, 45

Natural ResourcesFund, 39
NAVPS (Net asset value per share), 51

Net asset value, 46, 47
  per share, 51, 69, 70, 142
Net redemptions, 6
Nikkea 225 stock average, 10
Nixon, Richard, 1972 election campaign, 8
No-load funds, 86

Objectives, personal, 82
October, 1987 crash, 9-10, 37, 47, 54, 126, 137
  stock funds, 22, 24
O'Donnell, Jim, 14
One-country funds, 41
Ontario Securities Commission (OSC), 73, 74, 88, 134
"Open-ended", 50
Options, 22
OSC (Ontario Securities Commission), 73, 74, 88, 134

Pension Finance Associates Limited, 104
Performance:
  of funds, 83-86, 92, 93
  of managers, 92, 93
  tables, 82
Personal objectives, 82
Philip, Prince, 107
Portfolio, 94
  investing, 113
  managers, 86, 104
  recommendations, 91
Power Financial Corporation, 12
Precious metal funds, 154, 157
Preferred shares, 32
Principal Group, 88
Principal Speculators Fund, 24
Pro-Fund, 61
Promoters, 11
Prospectus, 89
Prudential Insurance Company of America, 135
Prudential-Bache Securities Canada Limited, 100

Ratio Withdrawal Plan, 72-73
Real estate funds, 37-39, 153, 157, 160
Real Property Trust, 38
Redeem shares, cost to, 69
Redemption:
  fees, 89
  of funds, 3
Regal Capital Planners Limited, 12, 61, 123-124
Registered Retirement Savings Plans (RRSP), 53-59
  contribution limits, 54
  eligible funds, 55, 141
    returns on, 164-167
  fees, 68
  investment strategy, 55
  investor profiles, 57-59
Rental income, 37
Residential loans, 30
Retirement strategy, 55
Revenue Canada, 76
  (*See also* Tax Reform 1987; Taxes)
Reward-risk ratio, 86, 142
Risk:
  factor, 85, 96, 137
  tolerance, 56, 82-83, 89
Royal Bank of Canada, 26, 136
Royal Trust Company, 43, 88, 137, 138
Royal Trust mortgage fund, 11-12
Royfund Equity Fund, 26, 57, 58, 87
RRIP eligible, 141
RRSP (Registered Retirement Savings Plans), 53-59

contribution limits, 54
eligible funds, 55, 141
returns on, 164-167
fees, 68
investment strategy, 55
investor profiles, 57-59

Sales, 11, 61, 62
agents, 6, 10, 12
ethics, 74
incentives, 74, 89-90
licensing, 75
responsibilities, 62-63
rewards, 14
charges, 9
fees, 62-63, 64, 89
literature, 75
Sarlos, Andy, 16
Saxon Group, 103, 137
Sceptre Investment Counsel Limited, 100
Schulich, Seymour, 93
ScotiaMcLeod:
bond index, 85
long-term government-bond index, 43
Scott, Geoffrey, 120
Scott, Michael, 120
Sector funds, 39-40
Securities:
registered, 70
regulators, 73
unregistered, 70
Service:
charges, 86
fees, 66, 68-69
Share prices, 100
Shareholder's meetings, 72
Short, Norman, 16
Short selling, 22
Shulman, Morton, 16
Siegerman, Martin, 26, 87
SilverFund, 39
Simple rate of return, 142
Spark, Peter, 41, 87, 111-114
Spooner, Mal, 97, 98
Standard and Poor's 500 index, 42-43
Stewart, Bob, 16
Stock funds, 19-23
restrictions, 22
Stock index fund, 42
Stock market crash, 1929, 47
Stock selling, 98-99
Stock-picking techniques, 97-98
Stone, Terry, 136
Summa Fund Limited, 36
Sun Life Assurance Company, 114, 135
Superstar phenomenon, 104
Survey of consumer attitudes, 133-134
Systematic withdrawal plans, 72-73

Tattersall, Bob, 10, 103, 136-137
Taurus Fund, 87
Tax reform, 1987, 32, 76, 138
Taxes, 76-80
TechnoFund, 39
Templeton, Dobbrow and Vance, 106
Templeton Emerging Nations Funds, 108
Templeton Foundation Prize for Progress in Religion, 107
Templeton, Galbraith and Hansberger Limited, 108
Templeton Global Growth Fund, 108
Templeton Growth Fund, 26, 41, 58, 66, 87, 95, 99, 101, 106
example of sales fee, 64
portfolio, 108
Templeton Income Fund, 108

Templeton International Group, 106
Templeton, John, 26, 87, 101, 102, 104, 106-108, 118
Templeton Management Incorporated, 58
Templeton Taft Philanthropic Trust, 108
Teresa, Mother, 108
Thompson, A.S., 100
Tillcan Financial Corporation, 123
"Top-down" approach, 23, 104
Toronto Stock Exchange 300
  Composite Index, 10, 21, 25, 42, 84
Toronto Stock Exchange Total Return Index, 40, 84
Toronto-Dominion Bank, 42
Total net assets, 142
Trafalgar Capital Management Corporation, 43, 103
Trailing commissions, 66
Transfer fees, 68
Trimark Canadian Fund, 57, 108
Trimark Fund, 108
Trimark Investment Management Incorporated, 53, 110-111

U.S.:
  equity funds, 154, 157, 160
  money market funds, 157
U.S. Securities and Exchange Commission Rule 12b-1, 67
United Accumulative Fund, 41
United Accumulative Retirement Fund, 83, 93
United Financial Managment, 41
United Venture Fund, 24
Up-front commission, 67

ValueFund, 39, 120
Vancity (Vancouver City Savings Credit Union), 36
Vancouver City Savings Credit Union (Vancity), 36
Vancouver Stock Exchange, 24
Variability, 83, 142
  ranking, 83
Venture capital funds, 138
Venture funds, 5-6
Vesco, Robert L., 7-9
Viking Commonwealth Fund, 93
Viking International Fund, 41

Walker, Wayne, 11, 134, 136, 137, 138
Walwyn Stodgell Cochran Murray Limited, 15, 125
Wealth, how to build, 132
Whiting, Richard, 15
William I, King of the Netherlands, 46
Windcroft Financial Planning Limited, 56
Woldring, Warren, 134
Wood Gundy Limited, 120, 127
  42nd street, 128

Yorkshire Trust Company, 120